# The Compleat Angler

## or the Contemplative Man's Recreation

IZAAK WALTON

"Simon Peter said, I go a fishing: and they said, We also will go with thee." JOHN xxi. 3.

INTRODUCTION BY
ANDREW LANG

DOVER PUBLICATIONS, INC.
Mineola, New York

*Bibliographical Note*

This Dover edition, first published in 2003, is an unabridged republication of the 1906 edition of the work published by J. M. Dent & Co., London, which includes Andrew Lang's Introduction to *The Compleat Angler* from his 1896 edition of the work. *The Compleat Angler* was first published in 1653.

*Library of Congress Cataloging-in-Publication Data*

Walton, Izaak, 1593–1683.
[Compleat angler]
The compleat angler, or, The contemplative man's recreation / Izaak Walton ; introduction by Andrew Lang.
p. cm.
Originally published: London : Printed by T. Maxey for R. Marriot, 1653.
Includes bibliographical references.
**ISBN-13: 978-0-486-43187-1 (pbk.)**
**ISBN-10: 0-486-43187-8 (pbk.)**
1. Fishing—Early works to 1800. I. Title: Compleat angler. II. Title: Contemplative man's recreation. III. Title.

SH433 .A2003
799.1'2—dc21

2003055308

Manufactured in the United States by RR Donnelley
43187806 2015
www.doverpublications.com

# Introduction

# Izaak Walton

by Andrew Lang

(An essay reprinted from his edition of *The Compleat Angler*, 1896)

To write on Walton is, indeed, to hold a candle to the sun. The editor has been content to give a summary of the chief, or rather the only known, events in Walton's long life, adding a notice of his character as displayed in his Biographies and in *The Compleat Angler*, with comments on the ancient and modern practice of fishing, illustrated by passages from Walton's foregoers and contemporaries. Like all editors of Walton,* he owes much to his predecessors, Sir John Hawkins, Oldys, Major, and, above all, to the learned Sir Harris Nicolas. The text here reprinted is, in the main, that of Sir Harris Nicolas, which was printed from Walton's Fifth Edition, 1676, the last that was revised by the author.

## HIS LIFE

The few events in the long life of Izaak Walton have been carefully investigated by Sir Harris Nicolas. All that can be extricated from documents by the alchemy of research has been selected, and I am unaware of any important acquisitions since Sir Harris Nicolas's second edition of 1860. Izaak was of an old family of Staffordshire yeomen, probably descendants of George Walton of Yoxhall, who died in 1571. Izaak's father was Jarvis Walton, who died in February 1595–6; of Izaak's mother nothing is known. Izaak himself was born at Stafford, on August 9, 1593, and was baptized on September 21. He died on December 15, 1683, having lived in the reigns of Elizabeth, James I., Charles I., under the Commonwealth, and under Charles II. The anxious and

*[See the last page of this Introduction for Lang's bibliographic note on Walton.—ed.]

changeful age through which he passed is in contrast with his very pacific character and tranquil pursuits.

Of Walton's education nothing is known, except on the evidence of his writings. He may have read Latin, but most of the books he cites had English translations. Did he learn his religion from "his mother or his nurse"? It will be seen that the free speculation of his age left him untouched: perhaps his piety was awakened, from childhood, under the instruction of a pious mother. Had he been orphaned of both parents (as has been suggested) he might have been less amenable to authority, and a less notable example of the virtues which Anglicanism so vainly opposed to Puritanism. His literary beginnings are obscure. There exists a copy of a work, *The Loves of Amos and Laura,* written by S. P., published in 1613, and again in 1619. The edition of 1619 is dedicated to "Iz. Wa.":—

"Thou being cause *it is as now it is*";

the Dedication does not occur in the one imperfect known copy of 1613. Conceivably the words, "as now it is" refer to the edition of 1619, which might have been emended by Walton's advice. But there are no emendations, hence it is more probable that Walton revised the poem in 1613, when he was a man of twenty, or that he merely advised the author to publish:—

"For, hadst thou held thy tongue, by silence might
These have been buried in oblivion's night."

S. P. also remarks:—

"No ill thing can be clothed in thy verse";

hence Izaak was already a rhymer, and a harmless one, under the Royal Prentice, gentle King Jamie.

By this time Walton was probably settled in London. A deed in the possession of his biographer, Dr. Johnson's friend, Sir John Hawkins, shows that, in 1614, Walton held half of a shop on the north side of Fleet Street, two doors west of Chancery Lane: the other occupant was a hosier. Mr. Nicholl has discovered that Walton was made free of the Ironmongers' Company on Nov. 12, 1618. He is styled an Ironmonger in his marriage licence. The facts are given in Mr. Marston's Life of Walton, prefixed to his edition of *The Compleat Angler* (1888). It is odd that a prentice ironmonger should have been a poet and a critic of poetry. Dr. Donne, before 1614, was Vicar of St. Dunstan's in the West, and in Walton had a parishioner, a disciple, and a friend. Izaak greatly loved the society of the clergy: he connected himself with Episcopal families, and had a natural taste for a Bishop. Through Donne, perhaps, or it may be in converse across the counter, he made acquaintance with Hales of Eton, Dr. King, and Sir Henry Wotton, himself an angler, and one who, like Donne and Izaak, loved a ghost story, and had several in his family. Drayton, the river-poet, author of the *Polyolbion*, is also spoken of by Walton as "my old deceased friend."

On Dec. 27, 1626, Walton married, at Canterbury, Rachel Floud, a niece, on the maternal side, by several descents, of Cranmer, the famous Archbishop of Canterbury. The Cranmers were intimate with the family of the judicious Hooker, and Walton was again connected with kinsfolk of that celebrated divine. Donne died in 1631, leaving to Walton, and to other friends, a bloodstone engraved with Christ crucified on an anchor: the seal is impressed on Walton's will. When Donne's poems were published in 1633, Walton added commendatory verses:—

> "As all lament
> (Or should) this general cause of discontent."

The parenthetic "or should" is much in Walton's manner. "Witness my mild pen, not used to upbraid the world," is also a pleasant and accurate piece of self-criticism. "I am his convert," Walton exclaims. In a citation from a manuscript which cannot be found, and perhaps never existed, Walton is spoken of as "a very sweet poet in his youth, and more than all in matters of love."[1] Donne had been in the same case: he, or Time, may have converted Walton from amorous ditties. Walton, in an edition of Donne's poems of 1635, writes of

> "This book (dry emblem) which begins
> With love; but ends with tears and sighs for sins."

The preacher and his convert had probably a similar history of the heart: as we shall see, Walton, like the Cyclops, had known love. Early in 1639, Wotton wrote to Walton about a proposed Life of Donne, to be written by himself, and hoped "to enjoy your own ever welcome company in the approaching time of the *Fly* and the *Cork*." Wotton was a fly-fisher; the cork, or float, or "trembling quill," marks Izaak for the bottom-fisher he was. Wotton died in December 1639; Walton prefixed his own Life of Donne to that divine's sermons in 1640. He says, in the Dedication of the reprint of 1658, that "it had the approbation of our late learned and eloquent King," the martyred Charles I. Living in, or at the corner of, Chancery Lane, Walton is known to have held parochial office: he was even elected "scavenger." He had the misfortune to lose seven children—of whom the last died in 1641—his wife,

[1]The MS. was noticed in *The Freebooter*, Oct. 18, 1823, but Sir Harris Nicolas could not find it, where it was said to be, among the Lansdowne MSS.

and his mother-in-law. In 1644 he left Chancery Lane, and probably retired from trade. He was, of course, a Royalist. Speaking of the entry of the Scots, who came, as one of them said, "for the goods,—and chattels of the English," he remarks, "I saw and suffered by it."[2] He also mentions that he "saw" shops shut by their owners till Laud should be put to death, in January 1645. In his Life of Sanderson, Walton vouches for an anecdote of "the knowing and conscientious King," Charles, who, he says, meant to do public penance for Strafford's death, and for the abolishing of Episcopacy in Scotland. But the condition, "peaceable possession of the Crown," was not granted to Charles, nor could have been granted to a prince who wished to reintroduce Bishops in Scotland. Walton had his information from Dr. Morley. On Nov. 25, 1645, Walton probably wrote, though John Marriott signed, an Address to the Reader, printed, in 1646, with Quarles's *Shepherd's Eclogues*. The piece is a little idyll in prose, and "angle, lines, and flies" are not omitted in the description of "the fruitful month of May," while Pan is implored to restore Arcadian peace to Britannia, "and grant that each honest shepherd may again sit under his own vine and fig-tree, and feed his own flock," when the King comes, no doubt. "About" 1646 Walton married Anne, half-sister of Bishop Ken, a lady "of much Christian meeknesse." Sir Harris Nicolas thinks that he only visited Stafford occasionally, in these troubled years. He mentions fishing in "Shawford brook"; he was likely to fish wherever there was water, and the brook flowed through land which, as Mr. Marston shows, he acquired about 1656. In 1650 a child was born to Walton in Clerkenwell; it died, but another, Isaac, was born in September 1651. In 1651 he published the *Reliquiae Wottonianae*, with a Memoir of Sir Henry Wotton. The knight had valued Walton's company as a cure for "those splenetic vapours that are called hypochondriacal."

Worcester fight was on September 3, 1651; the king was defeated, and fled, escaping, thanks to a stand made by Wogan, and to the loyalty of Mistress Jane Lane, and of many other faithful adherents. A jewel of Charles's, the lesser George, was preserved by Colonel Blague, who intrusted it to Mr. Barlow of Blore Pipe House, in Staffordshire. Mr. Barlow gave it to Mr. Milward, a Royalist prisoner in Stafford, and he, in turn, intrusted it to Walton, who managed to convey it to Colonel Blague in the Tower. The colonel escaped and the George was given back to the king. Ashmole, who tells the story, mentions Walton as "well beloved of all good men." This incident is, perhaps, the only known adventure in the long life of old Izaak. The peaceful angler, with a royal jewel in his pocket, must have encountered many dangers

---

[2]The quip about "goods and chattels" was revived later, in the case of a royal mistress.

on the highway. He was a man of sixty when he published his *Compleat Angler* in 1653, and so secured immortality. The quiet beauties of his manner in his various biographies would only have made him known to a few students, who could never have recognised Byron's "quaint, old, cruel coxcomb" in their author. "The whole discourse is a kind of picture of my own disposition, at least of my disposition in such days and times as I allow myself when honest Nat. and R. R. and I go a-fishing together." Izaak speaks of the possibility that his book may reach a second edition. There are now editions more than a hundred! Waltonians should read Mr. Thomas Westwood's Preface to his *Chronicle of the Compleat Angler*: it is reprinted in Mr. Marston's edition. Mr. Westwood learned to admire Walton at the feet of Charles Lamb:—

"No fisher,
But a well-wisher
To the game,"

as Scott describes himself.[3]

Lamb recommended Walton to Coleridge; "it breathes the very spirit of innocence, purity, and simplicity of heart; . . . it would sweeten a man's temper at any time to read it; it would Christianise every angry, discordant passion; pray make yourself acquainted with it." (Oct. 28, 1796.) According to Mr. Westwood, Lamb had "an early copy," found in a repository of marine stores, but not, even then, to be bought a bargain. Mr. Westwood fears that Lamb's copy was only Hawkins's edition of 1760. The original is extremely scarce. Mr. Locker had a fine copy; there is another in the library of Dorchester House: both are in their primitive livery of brown sheep, or calf. The book is one which only the wealthy collector can hope, with luck, to call his own. A small octavo, sold at eighteen-pence, *The Compleat Angler* was certain to be thumbed into nothingness, after enduring much from May showers, July suns, and fishy companionship. It is almost a wonder that any examples of Walton's and Bunyan's first editions have survived into our day. The little volume was meant to find a place in the bulging pockets of anglers, and was well adapted to that end. The work should be reprinted in a similar *format*: quarto editions are out of place.

[3]Sir Walter was fond of trout-fishing, and in his *Quarterly* review of Davy's *Salmonia*, describes his pleasure in wading Tweed, in "Tom Fool's light" at the end of a hot summer day. In salmon-fishing he was no expert, and said to Lockhart that he must have Tom Purdie to aid him in his review of *Salmonia*. The picturesqueness of salmon-spearing by torchlight seduced Scott from the legitimate sport.

The fortunes of the book, the *fata libelli*, have been traced by Mr. Westwood. There are several misprints* (later corrected) in the earliest copies, as (p. 88) "Fordig" for "Fordidg," (p. 152) "Pudoch" for "Pudock." The appearance of the work was advertised in *The Perfect Diurnal* (May 9–16), and in No. 154 of *The Mercurius Politicus* (May 19–26), also in an almanack for 1654. Izaak, or his publisher Marriott, cunningly brought out the book at a season when men expect the Mayfly. Just a month before, Oliver Cromwell had walked into the House of Commons, in a plain suit of black clothes, with grey stockings. His language, when he spoke, was reckoned unparliamentary (as it undeniably was), and he dissolved the Long Parliament. While Marriott was advertising Walton's work, Cromwell was making a Parliament of Saints, "faithful, fearing God, and hating covetousness." This is a good description of Izaak, but he was not selected. In the midst of revolutions came *The Compleat Angler* to the light, a possession for ever. Its original purchasers are not likely to have taken a hand in Royalist plots or saintly conventicles. They were peaceful men. A certain Cromwellian trooper, Richard Franck, was a better angler than Walton, and he has left to us the only contemporary and contemptuous criticism of his book: to this we shall return, but anglers, as a rule, unlike Franck, must have been for the king, and on Izaak's side in controversy.

Walton brought out a second edition in 1655. He rewrote the book, adding more than a third, suppressing *Viator*, and introducing *Venator*. New plates were added, and, after the manner of the time, commendatory verses. A third edition appeared in 1661, a fourth (published by Simon Gape, not by Marriott) came out in 1664, a fifth in 1668 (counting Gape's of 1664 as a new edition), and in 1676, the work, with treatises by Venables and Charles Cotton, was given to the world as *The Universal Angler.* Five editions in twelve years is not bad evidence of Walton's popularity. But times now altered. Walton is really an Elizabethan: he has the quaint freshness, the apparently artless music of language of the great age. He is a friend of "country contents": no lover of the town, no keen student of urban ways and mundane men. A new taste, modelled on that of the wits of Louis XIV., had come in: we are in the period of Dryden, and approaching that of Pope.

There was no new edition of Walton till Moses Browne (by Johnson's desire) published him, with "improvements," in 1750. Then came Hawkins's edition in 1760. Johnson said of Hawkins, "Why, ma'am, I believe him to be an honest man at the bottom; but, to be sure, he is penurious, and he is mean, and it must be owned he has a degree of brutality, and a tendency to savageness, that cannot easily be defended."

*[These page references to misprints point to earlier editions of Walton's *Compleat Angler*—not to this 1906 version of the work.—ed.]

This was hardly the editor for Izaak! However, Hawkins, probably by aid of Oldys the antiquary (as Mr. Marston shows), laid a good foundation for a biography of Walton. Errors he made, but Sir Harris Nicolas has corrected them. Johnson himself reckoned Walton's *Lives* as "one of his most favourite books." He preferred the life of Donne, and justly complained that Walton's story of Donne's vision of his absent wife had been left out of a modern edition. He explained Walton's friendship with persons of higher rank by his being "a great panegyrist."

The eighteenth century, we see, came back to Walton, as the nineteenth has done. He was precisely the author to suit Charles Lamb. He was reprinted again and again, and illustrated by Stoddart and others. Among his best editors are Major (1839), "Ephemera" (1853), Nicolas (1836, 1860), and Mr. Marston (1888).

The only contemporary criticism known to me is that of Richard Franck, who had served with Cromwell in Scotland, and, not liking the aspect of changing times, returned to the north, and fished from the Esk to Strathnaver. In 1658 he wrote his *Northern Memoirs*, an itinerary of sport, heavily cumbered by dull reflections and pedantic style. Franck, however, was a practical angler, especially for salmon, a fish of which Walton knew nothing: he also appreciated the character of the great Montrose. He went to America, wrote a wild cosmogonic work, and *The Admirable and Indefatigable Adventures of the Nine Pious Pilgrims* (one pilgrim catches a trout!) (London, 1708). The *Northern Memoirs* of 1658 were not published till 1694. Sir Walter Scott edited a new issue, in 1821, and defended Izaak from the strictures of the salmon-fisher. Izaak, says Franck, "lays the stress of his arguments upon other men's observations, wherewith he stuffs his indigested octavo; so brings himself under the angler's censure and the common calamity of a plagiary, to be pitied (poor man) for his loss of time, in scribbling and transcribing other men's notions. . . . I remember in Stafford, I urged his own argument upon him, that pickerel weed of itself breeds pickerel (pike)." Franck proposed a rational theory, "which my Compleat Angler no sooner deliberated, but dropped his argument, and leaves Gesner to defend it, so huffed away. . . ." "So note, the true character of an industrious angler more deservedly falls upon Merrill and Faulkner, or rather Izaak Ouldham, a man that fished salmon with but three hairs at hook, whose collections and experiments were lost with himself,"—a matter much to be regretted. It will be observed, of course, that hair was then used, and gut is first mentioned for angling purposes by Mr. Pepys. Indeed, the flies which Scott was hunting for when he found the lost MS. of the first part of *Waverley* are tied on horse-hairs. They are in the possession of the descendants of Scott's friend, Mr. William Laidlaw. The curious angler, consulting Franck, will find that his salmon flies are much like our own, but less variegated. Scott justly remarks that, while Walton was habit and repute a bait-fisher, even Cotton knows nothing of salmon. Scott wished that Walton had made the northern tour, but Izaak would have been sadly to seek, running after a fish down a gorge of the Shin or the Brora, and the discomforts of the north would have finished his career. In Scotland he would not have found fresh sheets smelling of lavender.

Walton was in London "in the dangerous year 1655." He speaks of his meeting Bishop Sanderson there, "in sad-coloured clothes, and, God knows, far from being costly." The friends were driven by wind and rain into "a cleanly house, where we had bread, cheese, ale, and a fire, for our ready money. The rain and wind were so obliging to me, as to force our stay there for at least an hour, to my great content and advantage; for in that time he made to me many useful observations of the present times with much clearness and conscientious freedom." It was a year of Republican and Royalist conspiracies: the clergy were persecuted and banished from London.

No more is known of Walton till the happy year 1660, when the king came to his own again, and Walton's Episcopal friends to their palaces. Izaak produced an "Eglog," on May 29:—

"The king! The king's returned! And now
Let's banish all sad thoughts, and sing:
We have our laws, and have our king."

If Izaak was so eccentric as to go to bed sober on that glorious twenty-ninth of May, I greatly misjudge him. But he grew elderly. In 1661 he chronicles the deaths of "honest Nat. and R. Roe,—they are gone, and with them most of my pleasant hours, even as a shadow that passeth away, and returns not." On April 17, 1662, Walton lost his second wife: she died at Worcester, probably on a visit to Bishop Morley. In the same year, the bishop was translated to Winchester, where the palace became Izaak's home. The Itchen (where, no doubt, he angled with worm) must have been his constant haunt. He was busy with his Life of Richard Hooker (1665). The peroration, as it were, was altered and expanded in 1670, and this is but one example of Walton's care of his periods. One beautiful passage he is known to have rewritten several times, till his ear was satisfied with its cadences. In 1670 he published his Life of George Herbert. "I wish, if God shall be so pleased, that I may be so happy as to die like him." In 1673, in a Dedication of the third edition of *Reliquiae Wottonianae*, Walton alludes to his friendship with a much younger and gayer man than himself, Charles Cotton (born 1630), the friend of Colonel Richard Lovelace, and of Sir John Suckling: the translator of Scarron's travesty of Virgil, and of

Montaigne's *Essays*. Cotton was a roisterer, a man at one time deep in debt, but he was a Royalist, a scholar, and an angler. The friendship between him and Walton is creditable to the freshness of the old man and to the kindness of the younger, who, to be sure, laughed at Izaak's heavily dubbed London flies. "In him," says Cotton, "I have the happiness to know the worthiest man, and to enjoy the best and the truest friend any man ever had." We are reminded of Johnson with Langton and Topham Beauclerk. Meanwhile Izaak the younger had grown up, was educated under Dr. Fell at Christ Church, and made the Grand Tour in 1675, visiting Rome and Venice. In March 1676 he proceeded M.A. and took Holy Orders. In this year Cotton wrote his treatise on fly-fishing, to be published with Walton's new edition; and the famous fishing house on the Dove, with the blended initials of the two friends, was built. In 1678, Walton wrote his Life of Sanderson. . . . "'Tis now too late to wish that my life may be like his, for I am in the eighty-fifth year of my age, but I humbly beseech Almighty God that my death may be; and do as earnestly beg of every reader to say Amen!" He wrote, in 1678, a preface to *Thealma and Clearchus* (1683). The poem is attributed to John Chalkhill, a Fellow of Winchester College, who died, a man of eighty, in 1679. Two of his songs are in *The Compleat Angler.* Probably the attribution is right: Chalkhill's tomb commemorates a man after Walton's own heart, but some have assigned the volume to Walton himself. Chalkhill is described, on the title-page, as "an acquaintant and friend of Edmund Spencer," which is impossible.[4]

On August 9, 1683, Walton wrote his will, "in the neintyeth year of my age, and in perfect memory, for which praised be God." He professes the Anglican faith, despite "a very long and very trew friendship for some of the Roman Church." His worldly estate he has acquired "neither by falsehood or flattery or the extreme crewelty of the law of this nation." His property was in two houses in London, the lease of Norington farm, a farm near Stafford, besides books, linen, and a hanging cabinet inscribed with his name, now, it seems, in the possession of Mr. Elkin Mathews. A bequest is made of money for coals to the poor of Stafford, "every last weike in Janewary, or in every first weike in Febrewary; I say then, because I take that time to be the hardest and most pinching times with pore people." To the Bishop of Winchester he bequeathed a ring with the posy, "A Mite for a Million." There are other bequests, including ten pounds to "my old friend, Mr. Richard Marriott," Walton's bookseller. This good man died in peace with his publisher, leaving him also a ring. A ring was left to a lady of the Portsmouth family, "Mrs. Doro. Wallop."

[4]There is an edition by Singer, with a frontispiece by Wainewright, the poisoner. London, 1820.

Walton died, at the house of his son-in-law, Dr. Hawkins, in Winchester, on Dec. 15, 1683: he is buried in the south aisle of the Cathedral. The Cathedral library possesses many of Walton's books, with his name written in them.[5] His *Eusebius* (1636) contains, on the flyleaf, repetitions, in various forms, of one of his studied passages. Simple as he seems, he is a careful artist in language.

Such are the scanty records, and scantier relics, of a very long life. Circumstances and inclination combined to make Walton choose the *fallentis semita vitae*. Without ambition, save to be in the society of good men, he passed through turmoil, ever companioned by content. For him existence had its trials: he saw all that he held most sacred overthrown; laws broken up; his king publicly murdered; his friends outcasts; his worship proscribed; he himself suffered in property from the raid of the Kirk into England. He underwent many bereavements: child after child he lost, but content he did not lose, nor sweetness of heart, nor belief. His was one of those happy characters which are never found disassociated from unquestioning faith. Of old he might have been the ancient religious Athenian in the opening of Plato's *Republic*, or Virgil's aged gardener. The happiness of such natures would be incomplete without religion, but only by such tranquil and blessed souls can religion be accepted with no doubt or scruple, no dread, and no misgiving. In his Preface to *Thealma and Clearchus* Walton writes, and we may use his own words about his own works: "The Reader will here find such various events and rewards of innocent Truth and undissembled Honesty, as is like to leave in him (if he be a good-natured reader) more sympathising and virtuous impressions, than ten times so much time spent in impertinent, critical, and needless disputes about religion." Walton relied on authority; on "a plain, unperplexed catechism." In an age of the strangest and most dissident theological speculations, an age of Quakers, Anabaptists, Antinomians, Fifth Monarchy Men, Covenanters, Independents, Gibbites, Presbyterians, and what not, Walton was true to the authority of the Church of England, with no prejudice against the ancient Catholic faith. As Gesner was his authority for pickerel weed begetting pike, so the Anglican bishops were security for Walton's creed.

To him, if we may say so, it was easy to be saved, while Bunyan, a greater humorist, could be saved only in following a path that skirted madness, and "as by fire." To Bunyan, Walton would have seemed a figure like his own Ignorance; a pilgrim who never stuck in the Slough of Despond, nor met Apollyon in the Valley of the Shadow, nor was captive in Doubting Castle, nor stoned in Vanity Fair. And of Bunyan,

[5] Nicolas, I. clv.

Walton would have said that he was among those Nonconformists who "might be sincere, well-meaning men, whose indiscreet zeal might be so like charity, as thereby to cover a multitude of errors." To Walton there seemed spiritual solace in remembering "that we have comforted and been helpful to a dejected or distressed family." Bunyan would have regarded this belief as a heresy, and (theoretically) charitable deeds "as filthy rags." Differently constituted, these excellent men accepted religion in different ways. Christian bows beneath a burden of sin; Piscator beneath a basket of trout. Let us be grateful for the diversities of human nature, and the dissimilar paths which lead Piscator and Christian alike to the City not built with hands. Both were seekers for a City which to have sought through life, in patience, honesty, loyalty, and love, is to have found it. Of Walton's book we may say:—

> *"Laudis amore tumes? Sunt certa piacula quae te*
> *Ter pure lecto poterunt recreare libello."*

## WALTON AS A BIOGRAPHER

It was probably by his *Lives*, rather than, in the first instance, by his *Angler*, that Walton won the liking of Dr. Johnson, whence came his literary resurrection. It is true that Moses Browne and Hawkins, both friends of Johnson's, edited *The Compleat Angler* before 1775–1776, when we find Dr. Horne of Magdalene, Oxford, contemplating a "benoted" edition of the *Lives*, by Johnson's advice. But the Walton of the *Lives* is, rather than the Walton of the *Angler*, the man after Johnson's own heart. The *Angler* is "a picture of my own disposition" on holidays. The *Lives* display the same disposition in serious moods, and in face of the eternal problems of man's life in society. Johnson, we know, was very fond of biography, had thought much on the subject, and, as Boswell notes, "varied from himself in talk," when he discussed the measure of truth permitted to biographers. "If a man is to write a *Panegyrick*, he may keep vices out of sight; but if he professes to write a *Life*, he must represent it as it really was." Peculiarities were not to be concealed, he said, and his own were not veiled by Boswell. "Nobody can write the life of a man but those who have eat and drunk and lived in social intercourse with him." "They only who live with a man can write his life with any genuine exactness and discrimination; and few people who have lived with a man know what to remark about him." Walton had lived much in the society of his subjects, Donne and Wotton; with Sanderson he had a slighter acquaintance; George Herbert he had only met; Hooker, of course, he had never seen in the flesh. It is obvious to every reader that his biographies of Donne and Wotton are his best. In Donne's Life he feels that he is writing of an English St. Austin,—"for I think none was so like him before his conversion; none so like St. Ambrose after it: and if his youth had the infirmities of the one, his age had the excellencies of the other; the learning and holiness of both."

St. Augustine made free confession of his own infirmities of youth. With great delicacy Walton lets Donne also confess himself, printing a letter in which he declines to take Holy Orders, because his course of life when very young had been too notorious. Delicacy and tact are as notable in Walton's account of Donne's poverty, melancholy, and conversion through the blessed means of gentle King Jamie. Walton had an awful loyalty, a sincere reverence for the office of a king. But wherever he introduces King James, either in his Donne or his Wotton, you see a subdued version of the King James of *The Fortunes of Nigel*. The pedantry, the good nature, the touchiness, the humour, the nervousness, are all here. It only needs a touch of the king's broad accent to set before us, as vividly as in Scott, the interviews with Donne, and that singular scene when Wotton, disguised as Octavio Baldi, deposits his long rapier at the door of his majesty's chamber. Wotton, in Florence, was warned of a plot to murder James VI. The duke gave him "such Italian antidotes against poison as the Scots till then had been strangers to": indeed, there is no antidote for a dirk, and the Scots were not poisoners. Introduced by Lindsay as "Octavio Baldi," Wotton found his nervous majesty accompanied by four Scottish nobles. He spoke in Italian; then, drawing near, hastily whispered that he was an Englishman, and prayed for a private interview. This, by some art, he obtained, delivered his antidotes, and, when James succeeded Elizabeth, rose to high favour. Izaak's suppressed humour makes it plain that Wotton had acted the scene for him, from the moment of leaving the long rapier at the door. Again, telling how Wotton, in his peaceful hours as Provost of Eton, intended to write a Life of Luther, he says that King Charles diverted him from his purpose to attempting a History of England "by a persuasive loving violence (to which may be added a promise of £500 a year)." He likes these parenthetic touches, as in his description of Donne, "always preaching to himself, like an angel from a cloud,—*but in none.*" Again, of a commendation of one of his heroes he says, "it is a known truth,—though it be in verse."

A memory of the days when Izaak was an amorist, and shone in love ditties, appears thus. He is speaking of Donne:—

> "Love is a flattering mischief . . . a passion that carries us to commit errors with as much ease as whirlwinds remove feathers."
>
> "The tears of lovers, or beauty dressed in sadness, are observed to have in them a charming sadness, and to become very often too strong to be resisted."

These are examples of Walton's sympathy: his power of portrait-drawing is especially attested by his study of Donne, as the young gallant and poet, the unhappy lover, the man of state out of place and neglected; the heavily burdened father, the conscientious scholar, the charming yet ascetic preacher and divine, the saint who, dying, makes himself, in his own shroud, an emblem of mortality.

As an example of Walton's style, take the famous vision of Dr. Donne in Paris. He had left his wife expecting her confinement:—

"Two days after their arrival there, Mr. Donne was left alone in that room in which Sir Robert and he, and some other friends, had dined together. To this place Sir Robert returned within half an hour, and as he left, so he found Mr. Donne alone, but in such an ecstacy, and so altered as to his looks, as amazed Sir Robert to behold him; insomuch that he earnestly desired Mr. Donne to declare what had befallen him in the short time of his absence. To which Mr. Donne was not able to make a present answer: but, after a long and perplexed pause, did at last say, 'I have seen a dreadful vision since I saw you: I have seen my dear wife pass twice by me through this room, with her hair hanging about her shoulders, and a dead child in her arms; this I have seen since I saw you.' To which Sir Robert replied, 'Sure, sir, you have slept since I saw you; and this is the result of some melancholy dream, which I desire you to forget, for you are now awake.' To which Mr. Donne's reply was, 'I cannot be surer that I now live than that I have not slept since I saw you: and I am as sure that at her second appearing she stopped, and looked me in the face, and vanished. . . .' And upon examination, the abortion proved to be the same day, and about the very hour, that Mr. Donne affirmed he saw her pass by him in his chamber.

". . . And though it is most certain that two lutes, being both strung and tuned to an equal pitch, and then one played upon, the other, that is not touched, being laid upon a table at a fit distance, will (like an echo to a trumpet) warble a faint audible harmony in answer to the same tune; yet many will not believe there is any such thing as a sympathy of souls, and I am well pleased that every reader do enjoy his own opinion. . . ."

He then appeals to authority, as of Brutus, St. Monica, Saul, St. Peter:—

"More observations of this nature, and inferences from them, might be made to gain the relation a firmer belief; but I forbear: lest I, that intended to be but a relator, may be thought to be an engaged person for the proving what was related to me, . . . by one who had it from Dr. Donne."

Walton was no Boswell; worthy Boswell would have cross-examined Dr. Donne himself.

Of dreams he writes:—

"Common dreams are but a senseless paraphrase on our waking thoughts, or of the business of the day past, or are the result of our over engaged affections when we betake ourselves to rest." . . . Yet "Almighty God (though the causes of dreams be often unknown) hath even in these latter times also, by a certain illumination of the soul in sleep, discovered many things that human wisdom could not foresee."

Walton is often charged with superstition, and the enlightened editor of the eighteenth century excised all the scene of Mrs. Donne's wraith as too absurd. But Walton is a very fair witness. Donne, a man of imagination, was, he tells us, in a perturbed anxiety about Mrs. Donne. The event was after dinner. The story is, by Walton's admission, at second hand. Thus, in the language of the learned in such matters, the tale is "not evidential." Walton explains it, if true, as a result of "sympathy of souls"—what is now called telepathy. But he is content that every man should have his own opinion. In the same way he writes of the seers in the Wotton family: "God did seem to speak to many of this family" (the Wottons) "in dreams," and Thomas Wotton's dreams "did usually prove true, both in foretelling things to come, and discovering things past." Thus he dreamed that five townsmen and poor scholars were robbing the University chest at Oxford. He mentioned this in a letter to his son at Oxford, and the letter, arriving just after the robbery, led to the discovery of the culprits. Yet Walton states the causes and nature of dreams in general with perfect sobriety and clearness. His tales of this sort were much to Johnson's mind, as to Southey's. But Walton cannot fairly be called "superstitious," granting the age in which he lived. Visions like Dr. Donne's still excite curious comment.

To that cruel superstition of his age, witchcraft, I think there is no allusion in Walton. Almost as uncanny, however, is his account of Donne's preparation for death:—

"Several charcoal fires being first made in his large study, he brought with him into that place his winding-sheet in his hand, and having put off all his clothes, had this sheet put on him, and so tied with knots at his head and feet, and his hands so placed as dead bodies are usually fitted, to be shrouded and put into their coffin or grave. Upon this urn he thus stood, with his eyes shut, and with so much of the sheet turned aside as might show his lean, pale, and death-like face, which was purposely turned towards the east, from which he expected the second coming of his and our Saviour Jesus. In this posture he was drawn at his just height, and, when the picture was fully finished, he caused it to be set by his bedside, where it continued, and became his hourly object till death."

Thus Donne made ready to meet the common fate:—

"That body, which once was a temple of the Holy Ghost, is now become a small quantity of Christian ashes. But I shall see it reanimated."

This is the very voice of Faith. Walton was, indeed, an assured believer, and to his mind, the world offered no insoluble problem. But we may say of him, in the words of a poet whom he quotes:—

"Many a one
Owes to his country his religion;
And in another would as strongly grow
Had but his nurse or mother taught him so."

In his account of Donne's early theological studies of the differences between Rome and Anglicanism, it is manifest that Izaak thinks these differences matters of no great moment. They are not for simple men to solve: Donne has taken that trouble for him; besides, he is an Englishman, and

"Owes to his country his religion."

He will be no Covenanter, and writes with disgust of an intruded Scots minister, whose first action was to cut down the ancient yews in the churchyard. Izaak's religion, and all his life, were rooted in the past, like the yew-tree. He is what he calls "the passive peaceable Protestant." "The common people in this nation," he writes, "think they are not wise unless they be busy about what they understand not, and especially about religion"; as Bunyan was busy at that very moment. In Walton's opinion, the plain facts of religion, and of consequent morality, are visible as the sun at noonday. The vexed questions are for the learned, and are solved variously by them. A man must follow authority, as he finds it established in his own country, unless he has the learning and genius of a Donne. To these, or equivalents for these in a special privy inspiration, "the common people" of his day, and ever since Elizabeth's day, were pretending. This was the inevitable result of the translation of the Bible into English. Walton quotes with approval a remark of a witty Italian on a populace which was universally occupied with Free-will and Predestination. The fruits Walton saw, in preaching Corporals, Antinomian Trusty Tompkinses, Quakers who ran about naked, barking, Presbyterians who cut down old yew-trees, and a Parliament of Saints. Walton took no kind of joy in the general emancipation of the human spirit. The clergy, he confessed, were not what he wished them to be, but they were better than Quakers, naked and ululant. To love God and his neighbour, and to honour the king, was Walton's unperplexed religion. Happily he was saved from the view of the errors and the fall of James II., a king whom it was not easy to honour. His social philosophy was one of established rank, tempered by equity and Christian charity. If anything moves his tranquil spirit, it is the remorseless greed of him who takes his fellow-servant by the throat and exacts the uttermost penny. How Sanderson saved a poor farmer from the greed of an extortionate landlord, Walton tells in his Life of the prelate, adding this reflection:—

"It may be noted that in this age there are a sort of people so unlike the God of mercy, so void of the bowels of pity, that they love only themselves and their children; love them so as not to be concerned whether the rest of mankind waste their days in sorrow or shame; people that are cursed with riches, and a mistake that nothing but riches can make them and theirs happy."

Thus Walton appears, this is "the picture of his own disposition," in the *Lives*. He is a kind of antithesis to John Knox. Men like Walton are not to be approached for new "ideas." They will never make a new world at a blow: they will never enable us to understand, but they can teach us to endure, and even to enjoy, the world. Their example is alluring:—

"Even the ashes of the just
Smell sweet, and blossom in the dust."

## THE COMPLEAT ANGLER

Franck, as we saw, called Walton "a plagiary." He was a plagiary in the same sense as Virgil and Lord Tennyson and Robert Burns, and, indeed, Homer, and all poets. *The Compleat Angler*, the father of so many books, is the child of a few. Walton not only adopts the opinions and advice of the authors whom he cites, but also follows the manner, to a certain extent, of authors whom he does not quote. His very exordium, his key-note, echoes (as Sir Harris Nicolas observes) the opening of A *Treatise of the Nature of God* (London, 1599). The *Treatise* starts with a conversation between a gentleman and a scholar: it commences:—

*Gent.* Well overtaken, sir!
*Scholar.* You are welcome, gentleman.

A more important source is *The Treatyse of Fysshynge wyth an Angle*, commonly attributed to Dame Juliana Barnes (printed at Westminster, 1496). A manuscript, probably of 1430–1450, has been published by Mr. Satchell (London, 1883). This book may be a translation of an unknown French original. It opens:—

"Soloman in hys paraboles seith that a glad spirit maket a flowryng age. That ys to sey, a feyre age and a longe" (like Walton's own), "and sith hyt ys so I aske this question, wyche bynne the menys and cause to reduce a man to a mery spryte." The angler "schall have hys holsom walke and mery at hys owne ease, and also many a sweyt eayr of divers erbis and flowres that schall make hym ryght hongre and well disposed in hys body. He schall heyr the melodies melodious of the ermony of byrde: he schall se also the yong swannes and signetes folowing ther eyrours, duckes, cootes, herons, and many other fowlys with ther brodys, wyche me semyt better then all the noyse of houndes, and blastes of hornes and other gamys that fawkners or hunters can make, and yf the angler take the fyssche, hardly then ys ther no man meryer then he in his sprites."

This is the very "sprite" of Walton; this has that vernal and matutinal air of opening European literature, full of birds' music, and redolent of dawn. This is the note to which the age following Walton would not listen.

In matter of fact, again, Izaak follows the ancient *Treatise*. We know his jury of twelve flies: the *Treatise* says:—

"These ben the xij flyes wyth whyche ye shall angle to the trought and graylling, and dubbe like as ye shall now here me tell.

"*Marche*. The donne fly, the body of the donne woll, and the wyngis of the pertryche. Another donne flye, the body of blacke woll, the wyngis of the blackyst drake; and the lay under the wynge and under the tayle."

Walton has:—

"The first is the dún fly in March: the body is made of dun wool, the wings of the partridge's feathers. The second is another dun fly: the body of black wool; and the wings made of the black drake's feathers, and of the feathers under his tail."

Again, the *Treatise* has:—

*Auguste*. The drake fly. The body of black wull and lappyd abowte wyth blacke sylke: winges of the mayle of the blacke drake wyth a blacke heed."

Walton has:—

"The twelfth is the dark drake-fly, good in August: the body made with black wool, lapt about with black silk, his wings are made with the mail of the black drake, with a black head."

This is word for word a transcript of the fifteenth century *Treatise*. But Izaak cites, not the ancient *Treatise*, but Mr. Thomas Barker.[6] Barker, in fact, gives many more, and more variegated flies than Izaak offers in the jury of twelve which he rendered, from the old *Treatise*, into modern English. Sir Harris Nicolas says that the jury is from Leonard Mascall's *Booke of Fishing with Hooke and Line* (London, 1609), but Mascall merely stole from the fifteenth-century book. In Cotton's practice, and that of *The Angler's Vade Mecum* (1681), flies were as numerous as among ourselves, and had, in many cases, the same names. Walton absurdly bids us "let no part of the line touch the water, but the fly only." Barker says, "Let the fly light first into the water." Both men insist on fishing down stream, which is, of course, the opposite of the true art, for fish lie with their heads up stream, and trout

[6]*Barker's Delight; or, The Art of Angling*. 1651, 1657, 1659, London.

are best approached from behind. Cotton admits of fishing both up and down, as the wind and stream may serve: and, of course, in heavy water, in Scotland, this is all very well. But none of the old anglers, to my knowledge, was a dry-fly fisher, and Izaak was no fly-fisher at all. He took what he said from Mascall, who took it from the old *Treatise*, in which, it is probable, Walton read, and followed the pleasant and to him congenial spirit of the mediæval angler. All these writers tooled with huge rods, fifteen or eighteen feet in length, and Izaak had apparently never used a reel. For salmon, he says, "some use a wheel about the middle of their rods or near their hand, which is to be observed better by seeing one of them, than by a large demonstration of words."

Mr. Westwood has made a catalogue of books cited by Walton in his *Compleat Angler*. There is Ælian (who makes the first known reference to fly-fishing); Aldrovandus, *De Piscibus* (1638); Dubravius, *De Piscibus* (1559); and the English translation (1599); Gerard's *Herball* (1633); Gesner, *De Piscibus* (*s.a.*) and *Historia Naturalis* (1558); Phil. Holland's *Pliny* (1601); Rondelet, *De Piscibus Marines* (1554); Silvianus, *Aquatilium Historiae* (1554): these nearly exhaust Walton's supply of authorities in natural history. He was devoted, as we saw, to authority, and had a childlike faith in the fantastic theories which date from Pliny. "Pliny hath an opinion that many flies have their birth, or being, from a dew that in the spring falls upon the leaves of trees." It is a pious opinion! Izaak is hardly so superstitious as the author of *The Angler's Vade Mecum*. I cannot imagine him taking "Man's fat and cat's fat, of each half an ounce, mummy finely powdered, three drams," and a number of other abominations, to "make an Oyntment according to Art, and when you Angle, anoint 8 inches of the line next the Hook therewith." Or, "Take the Bones and Scull of a Dead-man, at the opening of a Grave, and beat the same into Pouder, and put of this Pouder in the Moss wherein you keep your Worms,—*but others like Grave Earth as well*." No doubt grave earth is quite as efficacious.

These remarks show how Izaak was equipped in books and in practical information: it follows that his book is to be read, not for instruction, but for human pleasure.

So much for what Walton owed to others. For all the rest, for what has made him the favourite of schoolboys and sages, of poets and philosophers, he is indebted to none but his Maker and his genius. That he was a lover of Montaigne we know; and, had Montaigne been a fisher, he might have written somewhat like Izaak, but without the piety, the perfume, and the charm. There are authors whose living voices, if we know them in the flesh, we seem to hear in our ears as we peruse their works. Of such was Mr. Jowett, sometime Master of Balliol College, a good man, now with God. It has ever seemed to me that friends of Walton must thus have heard his voice as they read him, and that it reaches us too, though faintly. Indeed, we have here "a kind of picture of his own disposition," as he tells us Piscator is the Walton whom honest Nat. and R. Roe and Sir Henry Wotton knew on fishing-days. The book is a set of confessions, without their commonly morbid turn. "I write not for money, but for pleasure," he says; methinks he drove no hard bargain with good Richard Marriott, nor was careful and troubled about royalties on his eighteenpenny book. He regards scoffers as "an abomination to mankind," for indeed even Dr. Johnson, who, a century later, set Moses Browne on reprinting *The Compleat Angler*, broke his jest on our suffering tribe. "Many grave, serious men pity anglers," says Auceps, and Venator styles them "patient men," as surely they have great need to be. For our toil, like that of the husbandman, hangs on the weather that Heaven sends, and on the flies that have their birth or being from a kind of dew, and on the inscrutable caprice of fish; also, in England, on the miller, who giveth or withholdeth at his pleasure the very water that is our element. The inquiring rustic who shambles up erect when we are lying low among the reeds, even he disposes of our fortunes, with whom, as with all men, we must be patient, dwelling ever—

> "With close-lipped Patience for our only friend,
> Sad Patience, too near neighbour of Despair."

O the tangles, more than Gordian, of gut on a windy day! O bitter east wind that bloweth down stream! O the young ducks that, swimming between us and the trout, contend with him for the blue duns in their season! O the hay grass behind us that entangles the hook! O the rocky wall that breaks it, the boughs that catch it; the drought that leaves the salmon-stream dry, the floods that fill it with turbid, impossible waters! Alas for the knot that breaks, and for the iron that bends; for the lost landing-net, and the gillie with the gaff that scrapes the fish! Izaak believed that fish could hear; if they can, their vocabulary must be full of strange oaths, for all anglers are not patient men. A malison on the trout that "bulge" and "tail," on the salmon that "jiggers," or sulks, or lightly gambols over and under the line. These things, and many more, we anglers endure meekly, being patient men, and a light world fleers at us for our very virtue.

Izaak, of course, justifies us by the example of the primitive Christians, and, in the manner of the age, drowns opposition in a flood of erudition, out of place, but never pedantic; futile, yet diverting; erroneous, but not dull.

"God is said to have spoken to a fish, but never to a beast." There is a modern Greek phrase, "By the first word of God, and the second of the fish." As for angling, "it is somewhat like poetry: men are to be born so"; and many are born to be both rhymers and anglers. But, unlike many poets, the angler resembles "the Adonis, or Darling of the Sea, so called because it is a loving and innocent fish," and a peaceful; "and truly, I think most anglers are so disposed to most of mankind."

Our Saviour's peculiar affection for fishermen is, of course, a powerful argument. And it is certain that Peter, James, and John made converts among the twelve, for "the greater number of them were found together, fishing, by Jesus after His Resurrection." That Amos was "a good-natured, plain fisherman," only Walton had faith enough to believe. He fixes gladly on mentions of hooks in the Bible, omitting Homer, and that excellent Theocritean dialogue of the two old anglers and the fish of gold, which would have delighted Izaak, had he known it; but he was no great scholar. "And let me tell you that in the Scripture, angling is always taken in the best sense," though Izaak does not dwell on Tobias's enormous capture. So he ends with commendations of angling by Wotton, and Davors (Dennys, more probably) author of *The Secrets of Angling* (1613). To these we may add Wordsworth, Thomson, Scott, Hogg, Stoddart, and many minor poets who loved the music of the reel.

Izaak next illustrates his idea of becoming mirth, which excludes "Scripture jests and lascivious jests," both of them highly distasteful to anglers. Then he comes to practice, beginning with chub, for which I have never angled, but have taken them by misadventure, with a salmon fly. Thence we proceed to trout, and to the charming scene of the milkmaid and her songs by Raleigh and Marlowe, "I think much better than the strong lines that are now in fashion in this critical age," for Walton, we have said, was the last of the Elizabethans, and the new times were all for Waller and Dryden. "Chevy Chace" and "Johnny Armstrong" were dear to Walton as to Scott, but through a century these old favourites were to be neglected, save by Mr. Pepys and Addison. Indeed, there is no more curious proof of the great unhappy change then coming to make poetry a mechanic art, than the circumstance that Walton is much nearer to us, in his likings, than to the men between 1670 and 1770. Gay was to sing of angling, but in "the strong lines that are now in fashion." All this while Piscator has been angling with worm and minnow to no purpose, though he picks up "a trout will fill six reasonable bellies" in the evening. So we leave them after their ale, "in fresh sheets that smell of lavender." Izaak's practical advice is not of much worth; we read him rather for sentences like this: "I'll tell you, scholar: when I sat last on this primrose bank, and looked down these meadows, I thought of them as Charles the Emperor did of the city of Florence, 'that they were too pleasant to be looked upon, but only on holy-days.'" He did not say, like Fox, when Burke spoke of "a seat under a tree, with a friend, a bottle, and a book," "Why a book?" Izaak took his book with him—a practice in which, at least, I am fain to imitate this excellent old man.

As to salmon, Walton scarcely speaks a true word about their habits, except by accident. Concerning pike, he quotes the theory that they are bred by pickerel weed, only as what "some think." In describing the use of frogs as bait, he makes the famous, or infamous, remark, "Use him as though you loved him . . . that he may live the longer." A bait-fisher *may* be a good man, as Izaak was, but it is easier for a camel to pass through the eye of a needle. As coarse fish are usually caught only with bait, I shall not follow Izaak on to this unholy and unfamiliar ground, wherein, none the less, grow flowers of Walton's fancy, and the songs of the old poets are heard. *The Compleat Angler*, indeed, is a book to be marked with flowers, marsh-marigolds and fritillaries, and petals of the yellow iris, for the whole provokes us to content, and whispers that word of the apostle, "Study to be quiet."

## FISHING THEN AND NOW

Since Maui, the Maori hero, invented barbs for hooks, angling has been essentially one and the same thing. South Sea islanders spin for fish with a mother-of-pearl lure which is also a hook, and answers to our spoon. We have hooks of stone, and hooks of bone; and a bronze hook, found in Ireland, has the familiar Limerick bend. What Homer meant by making anglers throw "the horn of an ox of the stall" into the sea, we can only guess; perhaps a horn minnow is meant, or a little sheath of horn to protect the line. Dead bait, live bait, and imitations of bait have all been employed, and Ælian mentions artificial Mayflies used, with a very short line, by the Illyrians.

But, while the same in essence, angling has been improved by human ingenuity. The Waltonian angler, and still more his English predecessors, dealt much in the home-made. The *Treatise* of the fifteenth century bids you make your "Rodde" of a fair staff even of a six foot long or more, as ye list, of hazel, willow, or "aspe" (ash?), and "beke hym in an ovyn when ye bake, and let him cool and dry a four weeks or more." The pith is taken out of him with a hot iron, and a yard of white hazel is similarly treated, also a fair shoot of blackthorn or crabtree for a top. The butt is bound with hoops of iron, the top is accommodated with a noose, a hair line is looped in the noose, and the angler is equipped. Splicing is not used, but the joints have holes to receive each other, and with this instrument "ye may walk, and there is no man shall wit whereabout ye go." Recipes are given for colouring and plaiting hair lines, and directions for forging hooks. "The smallest quarell needles" are used for the tiniest hooks.

Barker (1651) makes the rod "of a hasel of one piece, or of two pieces set together in the most convenient manner, light and gentle." He recommends the use of a single hair next the fly,—"you shall have more rises," which is true, "and kill more fish," which is not so likely. The most delicate striking is required with fine gut, and with a single hair there must be many breakages. For salmon, Barker uses a rod ten feet in the butt, "that will carry a top of six foot pretty stiffe and strong." The "winder," or reel, Barker illustrates with a totally unintelligible design. His salmon fly "carries six wings"; perhaps he only means wings composed of six kinds of feathers, but here Franck is a better authority, his flies being sensible and sober in colour. Not many old salmon flies are in existence, nor have I seen more ancient specimens than a few, chiefly of peacocks' feathers, in the fly-leaf of a book at Abbotsford; they were used in Ireland by Sir Walter Scott's eldest son. The controversy as to whether fish can distinguish colours was unknown to our ancestors. I am inclined to believe that, for salmon, size, and perhaps shade, light or dark, with more or less of tinsel, are the only important points. Izaak stumbled on the idea of Mr. Stewart (author of *The Practical Angler*) saying, "for the generality, three or four flies, neat, and rightly made, and not too big, serve for a trout in most rivers, all the summer." Our ancestors, though they did not fish with the dry fly, were intent on imitating the insect on the water. As far as my own experience goes, if trout are feeding on duns, one dun will take them as well as another, if it be properly presented. But my friend Mr. Charles Longman tells me that, after failing with two trout, he examined the fly on the water, an olive dun, and found in his book a fly which exactly matched the natural insect in colour. With this he captured his brace.

Such incidents look as if trout were particular to a shade, but we can never be certain that the angler did not make an especially artful and delicate cast when he succeeded. Sir Herbert Maxwell intends to make the experiment of using duns of impossible and unnatural colours; if he succeeds with these, on several occasions, as well as with orthodox flies, perhaps we may decide that trout do not distinguish hues. On a Sutherland loch, an angler found that trout would take flies of any colour, except that of a light-green leaf of a tree. This rejection decidedly looked as if even Sutherland loch trout exercised some discrimination. Often, on a loch, out of three flies they will favour one, and that, perhaps, not the trail fly. The best rule is: when you find a favourite fly on a salmon river, use it: its special favouritism may be a superstition, but, at all events, salmon do take it. We cannot afford to be always making experiments, but Mr. Herbert Spencer, busking his flies the reverse way, used certainly to be at least as successful with sea trout as his less speculative neighbours in Argyllshire.

In making rods, Walton is most concerned with painting them: "I think a good top is worth preserving, or I had not taken care to keep a top above twenty years." Cotton prefers rods "made in Yorkshire," having advanced from the home-made stage. His were spliced, and kept up all through the season, as he had his water at his own door, while Walton trudged to the Lee and other streams near London, when he was not fishing the Itchen, or Shawford Brook. *The Angler's Vade Mecum* recommends eighteen-feet rods: preferring a fir butt, fashioned by the arrow-maker, a hazel top, and a tip of whalebone. This authority, even more than Walton, deals in mysterious "Oyntments" of gum ivy, horse-leek, asafœtida, man's fat, cat's fat, powdered skulls, and grave earth. A ghoulish body is the angler of the *Vade Mecum*. He recommends up-stream fishing, with worm, in a clear water, and so is a predecessor of Mr. Stewart. "When you have hooked a good fish, have an especial care to keep the rod bent, lest he run to the end of the line" (he means, as does Walton, lest he pull the rod horizontal) "and break either hook or hold." An old owner of my copy adds, in manuscript, "And hale him not to near ye top of the water, lest in flaskering he break ye line."

This is a favourite device of sea trout, which are very apt to "flasker" on the top of the water. The *Vade Mecum*, in advance of Walton on this point, recommends a swivel in minnow-fishing: but has no idea of an artificial minnow of silk. I have known an ingenious lady who, when the bodies of her phantom minnows gave out, in Norway, supplied their place successfully with bed-quilting artfully sewn. In fact, anything bright and spinning will allure fish, though in the upper Ettrick, where large trout exist, they will take the natural, but perhaps never the phantom or angel minnow. I once tried a spinning Alexandra fly over some large pond trout. They followed it eagerly, but never took hold, on the first day; afterwards they would not look at it at all. The *Vade Mecum* man, like Dr. Hamilton, recommends a light fly for a light day, a dark fly for a dark day and dark weather; others hold the converse opinion. Every one agrees that the smallness of the flies should be in proportion to the lowness of the water and the advance of summer.[7]

Our ancestors, apparently, used only one fly at a time; in rapid rivers,

[7]I have examined all the Angling works of the period known to me. Gilbert's *Angler's Delight* (1676) is a mere pamphlet; William Gilbert, gent., pilfers from Walton, without naming him, and has literally nothing original or meritorious. The book is very scarce. My own copy is "uncut," but incomplete, lacking the directions for fishing "in Hackney River." Gervase Markham, prior to Walton, is a compiler rather than an original authority on angling.

with wet fly, two, three, or, in lochs like Loch Leven, even four are employed. To my mind more than two only cause entanglements of the tackle. The old English anglers knew, of course, little or nothing of loch fishing, using bait in lakes. The great length of their rods made reels less necessary, and they do not seem to have waded much. A modern angler, casting upwards, from the middle of the stream, with a nine-foot rod, would have astonished Walton. They dealt with trout less educated than ours, and tooled with much coarser and heavier implements. They had no fine scruples about bait of every kind, any more than the Scots have, and Barker loved a lob-worm, fished on the surface, in a dark night. He was a pot-fisher, and had been a cook. He could catch a huge basket of trout, and dress them in many different ways,—broyled, calvored hot with antchovaes sauce, boyled, soused, stewed, fried, battered with eggs, roasted, baked, calvored cold, and marilled, or potted, also marrionated. Barker instructs my Lord Montague to fish with salmon roe, a thing prohibited and very popular in Scotland. "If I had known it but twenty years agoe, I would have gained a hundred pounds onely with that bait. I am bound in duty to divulge it to your Honour, and not to carry it to my grave with me. I do desire that men of quality should have it that delight in that pleasure: the greedy angler will murmur at me, but for that I care not." Barker calls salmon roe "an experience I have found of late: the best bait for a trout that I have seen in all my time," and it *is* the most deadly, in the eddy of a turbid water. Perhaps trout would take caviare, which is not forbidden by the law of the land. Any unscrupulous person may make the experiment, and argue the matter out with the water-bailie. But, in my country, it is more usual to duck that official, and go on netting, sniggling, salmon-roeing, and destroying sport in the sacred name of Liberty.

Scots wha fish wi' salmon roe,
Scots wha sniggle as ye go,
Wull ye stand the Bailie? No!
  Let the limmer die!

Now's the day and now's the time,
Poison a' the burns wi' lime,
Fishing fair's a dastard crime,
  We're for fishing *free!*

"Ydle persones sholde have but lyttyl mesure in the sayd disporte of fysshyng," says our old *Treatise*, but in southern Scotland they have left few fish to dysporte with, and the trout is like to become an extinct animal. Izaak would especially have disliked Fishing Competitions, which, by dint of the multitude of anglers, turn the contemplative man's recreation into a crowded skirmish; and we would repeat his remark, "the rabble herd themselves together" (a dozen in one pool, often), "and endeavour to govern and act in spite of authority."

For my part, had I a river, I would gladly let all honest anglers that use the fly cast line in it, but, where there is no protection, then nets, poison, dynamite, slaughter of fingerlings, and unholy baits devastate the fish, so that "Free Fishing" spells no fishing at all. This presses most hardly on the artisan who fishes fair, a member of a large class with whose pastime only a churl would wish to interfere. We are now compelled, if we would catch fish, to seek Tarpon in Florida, Mahseer in India; it does not suffice to "stretch our legs up Tottenham Hill."

ANDREW LANG

The following is a list of Walton's works:—

Life of Donne (prefixed to Sermons), 1640; issued separately, 1658. Life of Sir Henry Wotton ("Reliquiae Wottonianae"), 1651, 1654, 1672, 1685. The Compleat Angler, or the Contemplative Man's Recreation, 1653; second edition (with alterations), 1655; 1661, 1668, 1676 (with second part by Cotton and third by Col. R. Venables). Life of Hooker, 1665; second edition prefixed to Hooker's "Ecclesiastical Polity," 1666; 1676, 1682. Life of George Herbert, 1670. Collected Edition of Lives, 1670, 1675. Life of Robert Sanderson, 1678. Of the numerous editions of "The Compleat Angler" may be noted: by Sir John Hawkins (with earliest biography), 1760 (many editions); Illustrated Edition (with biography), by Sir Nicholas Harris Nicolas, 1836; by R. B. Marston (with life), 1888; Tercentenary, J. E. Harting, 1893; by Andrew Lang, 1896. The "Lives," Ed. A. H. Bullen (Bohn), 1884; Austin Dobson (Temple Classics), 1898.

Being a Diſcourſe of

# FISH and FISHING,

Not unworthy the peruſal of moſt *Anglers*.

---

Simon Peter *ſaid, I go a fiſhing: and they ſaid, We alſo wil go with thee.* John 21.3.

---

*London*, Printed by *T. Maxey* for RICH. MARRIOT, in S. *Dunſtans* Church-yard Fleetſtreet, 1653.

*To the Right worshipful*

# John Offley

*of Madeley Manor, in the County of Stafford*
*Esquire, My most honoured Friend*

SIR,—I have made so ill use of your former favours, as by them to be encouraged to entreat, that they may be enlarged to the patronage and protection of this Book: and I have put on a modest confidence, that I shall not be denied, because it is a discourse of Fish and Fishing, which you know so well, and both love and practice so much.

You are assured, though there be ignorant men of another belief, that Angling is an Art: and you know that Art better than others; and that this is truth is demonstrated by the fruits of that pleasant labour which you enjoy, when you purpose to give rest to your mind, and divest yourself of your more serious business, and, which is often, dedicate a day or two to this recreation.

At which time, if common Anglers should attend you, and be eye-witnesses of the success, not of your fortune, but your skill, it would doubtless beget in them an emulation to be like you, and that emulation might beget an industrious diligence to be so; but I know it is not attainable by common capacities: and there be now many men of great wisdom, learning, and experience, which love and practice this Art, that know I speak the truth.

Sir, this pleasant curiosity of Fish and Fishing, of which you are so great a master, has been thought worthy the pens and practices of divers in other nations, that have been reputed men of great learning and wisdom. And amongst those of this nation, I remember Sir Henry Wotton, a dear lover of this Art, has told me, that his intentions were to write a Discourse of the Art, and in praise of Angling; and doubtless he had done so, if death had not prevented him; the remembrance of which had often made me sorry, for if he had lived to do it, then the unlearned Angler had seen some better treatise of this Art, a treatise that might have proved worthy his perusal, which, though some have undertaken, I could never yet see in English.

But mine may be thought as weak, and as unworthy of common view; and I do here freely confess, that I should rather excuse myself, than censure others, my own discourse being liable to so many exceptions; against which you, Sir, might make this one, that it can contribute nothing to YOUR knowledge. And lest a longer epistle may diminish your pleasure, I shall make this no longer than to add this following truth, that I am really, Sir, your most affectionate Friend, and most humble Servant,

IZ. WA.

# CONTENTS

# THE EPISTLE TO THE READER

*To all Readers of this discourse, but especially to the honest Angler*

I THINK fit to tell thee these following truths; that I did neither undertake, nor write, nor publish, and much less own, this Discourse to please myself: and, having been too easily drawn to do all to please others, as I propose not the gaining of credit by this undertaking, so I would not willingly lose any part of that to which I had a just title before I began it; and do therefore desire and hope, if I deserve not commendations, yet I may obtain pardon.

And though this Discourse may be liable to some exceptions, yet I cannot doubt but that most Readers may receive so much pleasure or profit by it, as may make it worthy the time of their perusal, if they be not too grave or too busy men. And this is all the confidence that I can put on, concerning the merit of what is here offered to their consideration and censure; and if the last prove too severe, as I have a liberty, so I am resolved to use it, and neglect all sour censures.

And I wish the Reader also to take notice, that in writing of it I have made myself a recreation of a recreation; and that it might prove so to him, and not read dull and tediously, I have in several places mixed, not any scurrility, but some innocent, harmless mirth, of which, if thou be a severe, sour-complexioned man, then I here disallow thee to be a competent judge; for divines say, there are offences given, and offences not given but taken.

And I am the willinger to justify the pleasant part of it, because though it is known I can be serious at seasonable times, yet the whole Discourse is, or rather was, a picture of my own disposition, especially in such days and times as I have laid aside business, and gone a-fishing with honest Nat. and R. Roe; but they are gone, and with them most of my pleasant hours, even as a shadow that passeth away and returns not.

And next let me add this, that he that likes not the book, should like the excellent picture of the Trout, and some of the other fish, which I may take a liberty to commend, because they concern not myself.

Next, let me tell the Reader, that in that which is the more useful part of this Discourse, that is to say, the observations of the nature and breeding, and seasons, and catching of fish, I am not so simple as not to know, that a captious reader may find exceptions against something said of some of these; and therefore I must entreat him to consider, that experience teaches us to know that several countries alter the time, and I think, almost the manner, of fishes' breeding, but doubtless of their being in season; as may appear by three rivers in Monmouthshire, namely, Severn, Wye, and Usk, where Camden observes, that in the river Wye, Salmon are in season from September to April; and we are certain, that in Thames and Trent, and in most other rivers, they be in season the six hotter months.

Now for the Art of catching fish, that is to say, How to make a man that was none to be an Angler by a book, he that undertakes it shall undertake a harder task than Mr. Hales, a most valiant and excellent fencer, who in a printed book called A *Private School of Defence* undertook to teach that art or science, and was laughed at for his labour. Not but that many useful things might be learned by that book, but he was laughed at because that art was not to be taught by words, but practice: and so must Angling. And note also, that in this Discourse I do not undertake to say all that is known, or may be said of it, but I undertake to acquaint the Reader with many things that are not usually known to every Angler; and I shall leave gleanings and observations enough to be made out of the experience of all that love and practice this recreation, to which I shall encourage them. For Angling may be said to be so like the Mathematicks, that it can never be fully learnt; at least not so fully, but that there will still be more new experiments left for the trial of other men that succeed us.

But I think all that love this game may here learn something that may be worth their money, if they be not poor and needy men: and in case they be, I then wish them to forbear to buy it; for I write not to get money, but for pleasure, and this Discourse boasts of no more, for I hate to promise much, and deceive the Reader.

And however it proves to him, yet I am sure I have found a high content in the search and conference of what is here offered to the Reader's view and censure. I wish him as much in the perusal of it, and so I might here take my leave; but will stay a little and tell him, that whereas it is said by many, that in fly-fishing for a Trout, the Angler must observe his twelve several flies for the twelve months of the year, I say, he that follows that rule, shall be as sure to catch fish, and be as wise, as he that makes hay by the fair days in an Almanack, and no surer; for those very flies that used to appear about, and on, the water in one month of the year, may the following year come almost a month sooner or later, as the same year proves colder or hotter: and yet, in the following Discourse, I have set down the twelve flies that are in reputation with many anglers; and they may serve to give him some observations concerning them. And he may note, that there are in Wales, and other countries, peculiar flies, proper to the particular place or country; and doubtless, unless a man makes a fly to counterfeit that very fly in that place, he is like to lose his labour, or much of it; but for the generality, three or four flies neat and rightly made, and not too big, serve for a Trout in most rivers, all the summer: and for winter fly-fishing it is as useful as an Almanack out of date. And of these, because as no man is born an artist, so no man is born an Angler, I thought fit to give thee this notice.

When I have told the reader, that in this fifth impression there are many enlargements, gathered both by my own observation, and the communication with friends, I shall stay him no longer than to wish him a rainy evening to read this following Discourse; and that if he be an honest Angler, the east wind may never blow when he goes a-fishing.

I. W.

# THE FIRST DAY

*A Conference betwixt an Angler, a Falconer, and a Hunter, each commending his Recreation*

## CHAPTER I

PISCATOR, VENATOR, AUCEPS

PISCATOR. You are well overtaken, Gentlemen! A good morning to you both! I have stretched my legs up Tottenham Hill to overtake you, hoping your business may occasion you towards Ware whither I am going this fine fresh May morning.

VENATOR. Sir, I, for my part, shall almost answer your hopes; for my purpose is to drink my morning's draught at the Thatched House in Hoddesden; and I think not to rest till I come thither, where I have appointed a friend or two to meet me: but for this gentleman that you see with me, I know not how far he intends his journey; he came so lately into my company, that I have scarce had time to ask him the question.

AUCEPS. Sir, I shall by your favour bear you company as far as Theobalds, and there leave you; for then I turn up to a friend's house, who mews a Hawk for me, which I now long to see.

VENATOR. Sir, we are all so happy as to have a fine, fresh, cool morning; and I hope we shall each be the happier in the others' company. And, Gentlemen, that I may not lose yours, I shall either abate or amend my pace to enjoy it, knowing that, as the Italians say, "Good company in a journey makes the way to seem the shorter."

AUCEPS. It may do so, Sir, with the help of good discourse, which, methinks, we may promise from you, that both look and speak so cheerfully: and for my part, I promise you, as an invitation to it, that I will be as free and open hearted as discretion will allow me to be with strangers.

VENATOR. And, Sir, I promise the like.

PISCATOR. I am right glad to hear your answers; and, in confidence you speak the truth, I shall put on a boldness to ask you, Sir, whether business or pleasure caused you to be so early up, and walk so fast? for this other gentleman hath declared he is going to see a hawk, that a friend mews for him.

VENATOR. Sir, mine is a mixture of both, a little business and more pleasure; for I intend this day to do all my business, and then bestow another day or two in hunting the Otter, which a friend, that I go to meet, tells me is much pleasanter than any other chase whatsoever: howsoever, I mean to try it; for to-morrow morning we shall meet a pack of Otter-dogs of noble Mr. Sadler's, upon Amwell Hill, who will be there so early, that they intend to prevent the sunrising.

PISCATOR. Sir, my fortune has answered my desires, and my purpose is to bestow a day or two in helping to destroy some of those villanous vermin: for I hate them perfectly, because they love fish so well, or rather, because they destroy so much; indeed so much, that, in my judgment all men that keep Otter-dogs ought to have pensions from the King, to encourage them to destroy the very breed of those base Otters, they do so much mischief.

VENATOR. But what say you to the Foxes of the Nation, would not you as willingly have them destroyed? for doubtless they do as much mischief as Otters do.

PISCATOR. Oh, Sir, if they do, it is not so much to me and my fraternity, as those base vermin the Otters do.

AUCEPS. Why, Sir, I pray, of what fraternity are you, that you are so angry with the poor Otters?

PISCATOR. I am, Sir, a Brother of the Angle, and therefore an enemy to the Otter: for you are to note, that we Anglers all love one another, and therefore do I hate the Otter both for my own, and their sakes who are of my brotherhood.

VENATOR. And I am a lover of Hounds; I have followed many a pack of dogs many a mile, and heard many merry Huntsmen make sport and scoff at Anglers.

AUCEPS. And I profess myself a Falconer, and have heard many grave, serious men pity them, it is such a heavy, contemptible, dull recreation.

PISCATOR. You know, Gentlemen, it is an easy thing to scoff at any art or recreation; a little wit mixed with ill nature, confidence, and malice, will do it; but though they often venture boldly, yet they are often caught, even in their own trap, according to that of Lucian, the father of the family of Scoffers:

Lucian, well skilled in scoffing, this hath writ,
Friend, that's your folly, which you think your wit:
This you vent oft, void both of wit and fear,
Meaning another, when yourself you jeer.

If to this you add what Solomon says of Scoffers, that they are an abomination to mankind, let him that thinks fit scoff on, and be a Scoffer still; but I account them enemies to me and all that love Virtue and Angling.

And for you that have heard many grave, serious men pity Anglers; let me tell you, Sir, there be many men that are by others taken to be serious and grave men, whom we contemn and pity. Men that are taken to be grave, because nature hath made them of a sour complexion; money-getting men, men that spend all their time, first in getting, and next, in anxious care to keep it; men that are condemned to be rich, and then always busy or discontented: for these poor rich-men, we Anglers pity them perfectly, and stand in no need to borrow their thoughts to think ourselves so happy. No, no, Sir, we enjoy a contentedness above the reach of such dispositions, and as the learned and ingenuous Montaigne says, like himself, freely, "When my Cat and I entertain each other with mutual apish tricks, as playing with a garter, who knows but that I make my Cat more sport than she makes me? Shall I conclude her to be simple, that has her time to begin or refuse, to play as freely as I myself have? Nay, who knows but that it is a defect of my not understanding her language, for doubtless Cats talk and reason with one another, that we agree no better: and who knows but that she pities me for being no wiser than to play with her, and laughs and censures my folly, for making sport for her, when we two play together?"

Thus freely speaks Montaigne concerning Cats; and I hope I may take as great a liberty to blame any man, and laugh at him too, let him be never so grave, that hath not heard what Anglers can say in the justification of their Art and Recreation; which I may again tell you, is so full of pleasure, that we need not borrow their thoughts, to think ourselves happy.

VENATOR. Sir, you have almost amazed me; for though I am no Scoffer, yet I have, I pray let me speak it without offence, always looked upon Anglers, as more patient, and more simple men, than I fear I shall find you to be.

PISCATOR. Sir, I hope you will not judge my earnestness to be impatience: and for my simplicity, if by that you mean a harmlessness, or that simplicity which was usually found in the primitive Christians, who were, as most Anglers are, quiet men, and followers of peace; men that were so simply wise, as not to sell their consciences to buy riches, and with them vexation and a fear to die; if you mean such simple men as lived in those times when there were fewer lawyers; when men might have had a lordship safely conveyed to them in a piece of parchment no bigger than your hand, though several sheets will not do it safely in this wiser age; I say, Sir, if you take us Anglers to be such simple men as I have spoke of, then myself and those of my profession will be glad to be so understood: But if by simplicity you meant to express a general defect in those that profess and practice the excellent Art of Angling, I hope in time to disabuse you, and make the contrary appear so evidently, that if you will but have patience to hear me, I shall remove all the anticipations that discourse, or time, or prejudice, have possessed you with against that laudable and ancient Art; for I know it is worthy the knowledge and practice of a wise man.

But, Gentlemen, though I be able to do this, I am not so unmannerly as to engross all the discourse to myself; and, therefore, you two having declared yourselves, the one to be a lover of Hawks, the other of Hounds, I shall be most glad to hear what you can say in the commendation of that recreation which each of you love and practice; and having heard what you can say, I shall be glad to exercise your attention with what I can say concerning my own recreation and Art of Angling, and by this means we shall make the way to seem the shorter: and if you like my motion, I would have Mr. Falconer to begin.

AUCEPS. Your motion is consented to with all my heart; and to testify it, I will begin as you have desired me.

And first, for the Element that I use to trade in, which is the Air, an element of more worth than weight, an element that doubtless exceeds both the Earth and Water; for though I sometimes deal in both, yet the air is most properly mine, I and my Hawks use that most, and it yields us most recreation. It stops not the high soaring of my noble, generous Falcon; in it she ascends to such a height, as the dull eyes of beasts and fish are not able to reach to; their bodies are too gross for such high elevations; in the Air my troops of Hawks soar up on high, and when they are lost in the sight of men, then they attend upon and converse with the Gods; therefore I think my Eagle is so justly styled Jove's servant in ordinary: and that very Falcon, that I am now going to see, deserves no meaner a title, for she usually in her flight endangers herself, like the son of Dædalus, to have her wings scorched by the sun's heat, she flies so near it, but her mettle makes her careless of danger; for she then heeds nothing, but makes her nimble pinions cut the fluid air, and so makes her highway over the steepest mountains and deepest rivers, and in her glorious career looks with contempt upon those high steeples and magnificent palaces which we adore and wonder at; from which height, I can make her to descend by a word from my mouth, which she both knows and obeys, to accept of meat from my hand, to own me for her Master, to go home with me, and be willing the next day to afford me the like recreation.

And more; this element of air which I profess to trade in, the worth of it is such, and it is of such necessity, that no creature whatsoever—not only those numerous creatures that feed on the face of the earth, but those various creatures that have their dwelling within the waters, every creature that hath life in its nostrils, stands in need of my element. The waters cannot preserve the Fish without air, witness the not breaking of ice in an extreme frost; the reason is, for that if the inspiring and expiring organ of any animal be stopped, it suddenly yields to nature, and dies. Thus necessary is air, to the existence both of Fish and Beasts, nay, even to Man himself; that air, or breath of life, with which God at first inspired mankind, he, if he wants it, dies presently, becomes a sad object to all that loved and beheld him, and in an instant turns to putrefaction.

Nay more; the very birds of the air, those that be not Hawks, are both so many and so useful and pleasant to mankind, that I must not let them pass without some observations. They both feed and refresh him; feed him with their choice bodies, and refresh him with their heavenly voices:—I will not undertake to mention the several kinds of Fowl by which this is done: and his curious palate pleased by day, and which with their very excrements afford him a soft lodging at night:—These I will pass by, but not those little nimble musicians of the air, that warble forth their curious ditties, with which nature hath furnished them to the shame of art.

As first the Lark, when she means to rejoice, to cheer herself and those that hear her; she then quits the earth, and sings as she ascends higher into the air, and having ended her heavenly employment, grows then mute, and sad, to think she must descend to the dull earth, which she would not touch, but for necessity.

How do the Blackbird and Thrassel with their melodious voices bid welcome to the cheerful Spring, and in their fixed months warble forth such ditties as no art or instrument can reach to!

Nay, the smaller birds also do the like in their particular seasons, as namely the Laverock, the Tit-lark, the little Linnet, and the honest Robin that loves mankind both alive and dead.

But the Nightingale, another of my airy creatures, breathes such sweet loud musick out of her little instrumental throat, that it might make mankind to think miracles are not ceased. He that at midnight, when the very labourer sleeps securely, should hear, as I have very often, the clear airs, the sweet descants, the natural rising and falling, the doubling and redoubling of her voice, might well be lifted above earth, and say, "Lord, what musick hast thou provided for the Saints in Heaven, when thou affordest bad men such musick on Earth!"

And this makes me the less to wonder at the many Aviaries in Italy, or at the great charge of Varro's Aviary, the ruins of which are yet to be seen in Rome, and is still so famous there, that it is reckoned for one of those notables which men of foreign nations either record, or lay up in their memories when they return from travel.

This for the birds of pleasure, of which very much more might be said. My next shall be of birds of political use. I think it is not to be doubted that Swallows have been taught to carry letters between two armies; but 'tis certain that when the Turks besieged Malta or Rhodes, I now remember not which it was, Pigeons are then related to carry and recarry letters: and Mr. G. Sandys, in his *Travels*, relates it to be done betwixt Aleppo and Babylon. But if that be disbelieved, it is not to be doubted that the Dove was sent out of the ark by Noah, to give him notice of land, when to him all appeared to be sea; and the Dove proved a faithful and comfortable messenger. And for the sacrifices of the law, a pair of Turtle-doves, or young Pigeons, were as well accepted as costly Bulls and Rams; and when God would feed the Prophet Elijah, after a kind of miraculous manner, he did it by Ravens, who brought him meat morning and evening. Lastly, the Holy Ghost, when he descended visibly upon our Saviour, did it by assuming the shape of a Dove. And, to conclude this part of my discourse, pray remember these wonders were done by birds of air, the element in which they, and I, take so much pleasure.

There is also a little contemptible winged creature, an inhabitant of my aerial element, namely the laborious Bee, of whose prudence, policy, and regular government of their own commonwealth, I might say much, as also of their several kinds, and how useful their honey and wax are both for meat and medicines to mankind; but I will leave them to their sweet labour, without the least disturbance, believing them to be all very busy at this very time amongst the herbs and flowers that we see nature puts forth this May morning.

And now to return to my Hawks, from whom I have made too long a digression. You are to note, that they are usually distinguished into two kinds; namely, the long-winged, and the short-winged Hawk: of the first kind, there be chiefly in use amongst us in this nation,

The Gerfalcon and Jerkin,
The Falcon and Tassel-gentle,
The Laner and Laneret,
The Bockerel and Bockeret,
The Saker and Sacaret,
The Merlin and Jack Merlin,
The Hobby and Jack:

There is the Stelletto of Spain,

The Blood-red Rook from Turkey,
The Waskite from Virginia:

And there is of short-winged Hawks,
The Eagle and Iron,
The Goshawk and Tarcel,
The Sparhawk and Musket,
The French Pye of two sorts:

These are reckoned Hawks of note and worth; but we have also of an inferior rank,
The Stanyel, the Ringtail,
The Raven, the Buzzard,
The Forked Kite, the Bald Buzzard,
The Hen-driver, and others that I forbear to name.

Gentlemen, if I should enlarge my discourse to the observation of the Eires, the Brancher, the Ramish Hawk, the Haggard, and the two sorts of Lentners, and then treat of their several Ayries, their Mewings, rare order of casting, and the renovation of their feathers: their reclaiming, dieting, and then come to their rare stories of practice; I say, if I should enter into these, and many other observations that I could make, it would be much, very much pleasure to me: but lest I should break the rules of civility with you, by taking up more than the proportion of time allotted to me, I will here break off, and entreat you, Mr. Venator, to say what you are able in the commendation of Hunting, to which you are so much affected; and if time will serve, I will beg your favour for a further enlargement of some of those several heads of which I have spoken. But no more at present.

VENATOR. Well, Sir, and I will now take my turn, and will first begin with a commendation of the Earth, as you have done most excellently of the Air; the Earth being that element upon which I drive my pleasant, wholesome, hungry trade. The Earth is a solid, settled element; an element most universally beneficial both to man and beast; to men who have their several recreations upon it, as horse-races, hunting, sweet smells, pleasant walks: the earth feeds man, and all those several beasts that both feed him, and afford him recreation. What pleasure doth man take in hunting the stately Stag, the generous Buck, the wild Boar, the cunning Otter, the crafty Fox, and the fearful Hare! And if I may descend to a lower game, what pleasure is it sometimes with gins to betray the very vermin of the earth; as namely, the Fichat, the Fulimart, the Ferret, the Pole-cat, the Mouldwarp, and the like creatures that live upon the face, and within the bowels of, the Earth. How doth the Earth bring forth herbs, flowers, and fruits, both for physick and the pleasure of mankind! and above all, to me at least, the fruitful vine, of which when I drink moderately, it clears my brain, cheers my heart, and sharpens my wit. How could Cleopatra have feasted Mark Antony with eight wild Boars roasted whole at one supper, and other meat suitable, if the earth had not been a bountiful mother? But to pass by the mighty Elephant, which the Earth breeds and nourisheth, and descend to the least of creatures, how doth the earth afford us a doctrinal example in the little Pismire, who in the summer provides and lays up her winter provision, and teaches man to do the like! The earth feeds and carries those horses that carry us. If I would be prodigal of my time and your patience, what might not I say in commendations of the earth? That puts limits to the proud and raging sea, and by that means preserves both man and beast, that it destroys them not, as we see it daily doth those that venture upon the sea, and are there shipwrecked, drowned, and left to feed Haddocks; when we that are so wise as to keep ourselves on earth, walk, and talk, and live, and eat, and drink, and go a hunting: of which recreation I will say a little, and then leave Mr. Piscator to the commendation of Angling.

Hunting is a game for princes and noble persons; it hath been highly prized in all ages; it was one of the qualifications that Xenophon bestowed on his Cyrus, that he was a hunter of wild beasts. Hunting trains up the younger nobility to the use of manly exercises in their riper age. What more manly exercise than hunting the Wild Boar, the Stag, the Buck, the Fox, or the Hare? How doth it preserve health, and increase strength and activity!

And for the dogs that we use, who can commend their excellency to that height which they deserve? How perfect is the hound at smelling, who never leaves or forsakes his first scent, but follows it through so many changes and varieties of other scents, even over, and in, the water, and into the earth! What music doth a pack of dogs then make to any man, whose heart and ears are so happy as to be set to the tune of such instruments! How will a right Greyhound fix his eye on the best Buck in a herd, single him out, and follow him, and him only, through a whole herd of rascal game, and still know and then kill him! For my hounds, I know the language of them, and they know the language and meaning of one another, as perfectly as we know the voices of those with whom we discourse daily.

I might enlarge myself in the commendation of Hunting, and of the noble Hound especially, as also of the docibleness of dogs in general; and I might make many observations of land-creatures, that for composition, order, figure, and constitution, approach nearest to the completeness and understanding of man; especially of those creatures, which Moses in the Law permitted to the Jews, which have cloven hoofs, and chew the cud; which I shall forbear to name, because I will not be so uncivil to Mr. Piscator, as not to allow him a time for the commendation of Angling, which he calls an art; but doubtless it is an easy one: and, Mr. Auceps, I doubt we shall hear a watery discourse of it, but I hope it will not be a long one.

AUCEPS. And I hope so too, though I fear it will.

PISCATOR. Gentlemen, let not prejudice prepossess you. I confess my discourse is like to prove suitable to my recreation, calm and quiet; we seldom take the name of God into our mouths, but it is either to praise him, or pray to him: if others use it vainly in the midst of their recreations, so vainly as if they meant to conjure, I must tell you, it is neither our fault nor our custom; we protest against it. But, pray remember, I accuse nobody; for as I would not make a "watery discourse," so I would not put too much vinegar into it; nor would I raise the reputation of my own art, by the diminution or ruin of another's. And so much for the prologue to what I mean to say.

And now for the Water, the element that I trade in. The water is the eldest daughter of the creation, the element upon which the Spirit of God did first move, the element which God commanded to bring forth living creatures abundantly; and without which, those that inhabit the land, even all creatures that have breath in their nostrils, must suddenly return to putrefaction. Moses, the great lawgiver and chief philosopher, skilled in all the learning of the Egyptians, who was called the friend of God, and knew the mind of the Almighty, names this element the first in the creation: this is the element upon which the Spirit of God did first move, and is the chief ingredient in the creation: many philosophers have made it to comprehend all the other elements, and most allow it the chiefest in the mixtion of all living creatures.

There be that profess to believe that all bodies are made of water, and may be reduced back again to water only; they endeavour to demonstrate it thus:

Take a willow, or any like speedy growing plant, newly rooted in a box or barrel full of earth, weigh them all together exactly when the tree begins to grow, and then weigh all together after the tree is increased from its first rooting, to weigh a hundred pound weight more than when it was first rooted and weighed; and you shall find this augment of the tree to be without the diminution of one drachm weight of the earth. Hence they infer this increase of wood to be from water of rain, or from dew, and not to be from any other element; and they affirm, they can reduce this wood back again to water; and they affirm also, the same may be done in any animal or vegetable. And this I take to be a fair testimony of the excellency of my element of water.

The water is more productive than the earth. Nay, the earth hath no fruitfulness without showers or dews; for all the herbs, and flowers, and fruit, are produced and thrive by the water; and the very minerals are fed by streams that run under ground, whose natural course carries them to the tops of many high mountains, as we see by several springs breaking forth on the tops of the highest hills; and this is also witnessed by the daily trial and testimony of several miners.

Nay, the increase of those creatures that are bred and fed in the water are not only more and more miraculous, but more advantageous to man, not only for the lengthening of his life, but for the preventing of sickness; for it is observed by the most learned physicians, that the casting off of Lent, and other fish days, which hath not only given the lie to so many learned, pious, wise founders of colleges, for which we should be ashamed, hath doubtless been the chief cause of those many putrid, shaking intermitting agues, unto which this nation of ours is now more subject, than those wiser countries that feed on herbs, salads, and plenty of fish; of which it is observed in story, that the greatest part of the world now do. And it may be fit to remember that Moses appointed fish to be the chief diet for the best commonwealth that ever yet was.

And it is observable, not only that there are fish, as namely the Whale, three times as big as the mighty Elephant, that is so fierce in battle, but that the mightiest feasts have been of fish. The Romans, in the height of their glory, have made fish the mistress of all their entertainments; they have had musick to usher in their Sturgeons, Lampreys, and Mullets, which they would purchase at rates rather to be wondered at than believed. He that shall view the writings of Macrobius, or Varro, may be confirmed and informed of this, and of the incredible value of their fish and fish-ponds.

But, Gentlemen, I have almost lost myself, which I confess I may easily do in this philosophical discourse; I met with most of it very lately, and, I hope, happily, in a conference with a most learned physician, Dr. Wharton, a dear friend, that loves both me and my art of Angling. But, however, I will wade no deeper into these mysterious arguments, but pass to such observations as I can manage with more pleasure, and less fear of running into error. But I must not yet forsake the waters, by whose help we have so many known advantages.

And first, to pass by the miraculous cures of our known baths, how advantageous is the sea for our daily traffick, without which we could not now subsist. How does it not only furnish us with food and physick for the bodies, but with such observations for the mind as ingenious persons would not want!

How ignorant had we been of the beauty of Florence, of the monuments, urns, and rarities that yet remain in and near unto old and new Rome, so many as it is said will take up a year's time to view, and afford to each of them but a convenient consideration! And therefore it is not to be wondered at, that so learned and devout a father as St. Jerome, after his wish to have seen Christ in the flesh, and to have heard St. Paul preach, makes his third wish, to have seen Rome in her glory; and that glory is not yet all lost, for what pleasure is it to see the monuments of Livy, the choicest of the historians; of Tully, the best of orators; and to see the bay trees that now grow out of the very tomb of Virgil! These, to any that love learning, must be pleasing. But what pleasure is it to a devout Christian, to see there the humble house in which St. Paul was content to dwell, and to view the many rich statues that are made in honour of his memory! nay, to see the very place in which St. Peter and he lie buried together! These are in and near to Rome. And how much more doth it please the pious curiosity of a Christian, to see that place, on which the blessed Saviour of the world was pleased to humble himself, and to take our nature upon him, and to converse with men: to see Mount Sion, Jerusalem, and the very sepulchre of our Lord Jesus! How may it beget and heighten the zeal of a Christian, to see the devotions that are daily paid to him at that place! Gentlemen, lest I forget myself, I will stop here, and remember you, that but for my element of water, the inhabitants of this poor island must remain ignorant that such things ever were, or that any of them have yet a being.

Gentlemen, I might both enlarge and lose myself in such like arguments. I might tell you that Almighty God is said to have spoken to a fish, but never to a beast; that he hath made a whale a ship, to carry and set his prophet, Jonah, safe on the appointed shore. Of these I might speak, but I must in manners break off, for I see Theobald's House. I cry you mercy for being so long, and thank you for your patience.

AUCEPS. Sir, my pardon is easily granted you: I except against nothing that you have said: nevertheless, I must part with you at this park-wall, for which I am very sorry; but I assure you, Mr. Piscator, I now part with you full of good thoughts, not only of yourself, but your recreation. And so, Gentlemen, God keep you both.

PISCATOR. Well, now, Mr. Venator, you shall neither want time, nor my attention to hear you enlarge your discourse concerning hunting.

VENATOR. Not I, Sir: I remember you said that Angling itself was of great antiquity, and a perfect art, and an art not easily attained to; and you have so won upon me in your former discourse, that I am very desirous to hear what you can say further concerning those particulars.

PISCATOR. Sir, I did say so: and I doubt not but if you and I did converse together but a few hours, to leave you possessed with the same high and happy thoughts that now possess me of it; not only of the antiquity of Angling, but that it deserves commendations; and that it is an art, and an art worthy the knowledge and practice of a wise man.

VENATOR. Pray, Sir, speak of them what you think fit, for we have yet five miles to the Thatched House; during which walk, I dare promise you, my patience and diligent attention shall not be wanting. And if you shall make that to appear which you have undertaken, first, that it is an art, and an art worth the learning, I shall beg that I may attend you a day or two a-fishing, and that I may become your scholar, and be instructed in the art itself which you so much magnify.

PISCATOR. O, Sir, doubt not but that Angling is an art; is it not an art to deceive a Trout with an artificial Fly? a Trout! that is more sharp-sighted than any Hawk you have named, and more watchful and timorous than your high-mettled Merlin is bold? and yet, I doubt not to catch a brace or two to-morrow, for a friend's breakfast: doubt not therefore, Sir, but that angling is an art, and an art worth your learning. The question is rather, whether you be capable of learning it? for angling is somewhat like poetry, men are to be born so: I mean, with inclinations to it, though both may be heightened by discourse and practice: but he that hopes to be a good angler, must not only bring an inquiring, searching, observing wit, but he must bring a large measure of hope and patience, and a love and propensity to the art itself; but having once got and practiced it, then doubt not but angling will prove to be so pleasant, that it will prove to be, like virtue, a reward to itself.

VENATOR. Sir, I am now become so full of expectation, that I long much to have you proceed, and in the order that you propose.

PISCATOR. Then first, for the antiquity of Angling, of which I shall not say much, but only this; some say it is as ancient as Deucalion's flood: others, that Belus, who was the first inventor of godly and virtuous recreations, was the first inventor of Angling: and some others say, for former times have had their disquisitions about the antiquity of it, that Seth, one of the sons of Adam, taught it to his sons, and that by them it was derived to posterity: others say that he left it engraven on those pillars which he erected, and trusted to preserve the knowledge of the mathematicks, musick, and the rest of that precious knowledge, and those useful arts, which by God's appointment or allowance, and his noble industry, were thereby preserved from perishing in Noah's flood.

These, Sir, have been the opinions of several men, that have possibly endeavoured to make angling more ancient than is needful, or may well be warranted; but for my part, I shall content myself in telling you, that angling is much more ancient than the incarnation of our Saviour; for in the Prophet Amos mention is made of fish-hooks; and in the book of Job, which was long before the days of Amos, for that book is said to have been written by Moses, mention is made also of fish-hooks, which must imply anglers in those times.

But, my worthy friend, as I would rather prove myself a gentleman, by being learned and humble, valiant and inoffensive, virtuous and communicable, than by any fond ostentation of riches, or, wanting those virtues myself, boast that these were in my ancestors; and yet I grant, that where a noble and ancient descent and such merit meet in any man, it is a double dignification of that person; so if this antiquity of angling, which for my part I have not forced, shall, like an ancient family, be either an honour or an ornament to this virtuous art which I profess to love and practice, I shall be the gladder that I made an accidental mention of the antiquity of it, of which I shall say no more, but proceed to that just commendation which I think it deserves.

And for that, I shall tell you, that in ancient times a debate hath risen, and it remains yet unresolved, whether the happiness of man in this world doth consist more in contemplation or action? Concerning which, some have endeavoured to maintain their opinion of the first; by saying, that the nearer we mortals come to God by way of imitation, the more happy we are. And they say, that God enjoys himself only, by a contemplation of his own infiniteness, eternity, power, and goodness, and the like. And upon this ground, many cloisteral men of great learning and devotion, prefer contemplation before action. And many of the fathers seem to approve this opinion, as may appear in their commentaries upon the words of our Saviour to Martha.

And on the contrary, there want not men of equal authority and credit, that prefer action to be the more excellent; as namely, experiments in physick, and the application of it, both for the ease and prolongation of man's life; by which each man is enabled to act and do good to others, either to serve his country, or do good to particular persons: and they say also, that action is doctrinal, and teaches both art and virtue, and is a maintainer of human society; and for these, and other like reasons, to be preferred before contemplation.

Concerning which two opinions I shall forbear to add a third, by declaring my own; and rest myself contented in telling you, my very worthy friend, that both these meet together, and do most properly belong to the most honest, ingenuous, quiet, and harmless art of angling.

And first, I shall tell you what some have observed, and I have found it to be a real truth, that the very sitting by the river's side is not only the quietest and fittest place for contemplation, but will invite an angler to it: and this seems to be maintained by the learned Peter du Moulin, who, in his discourse of the fulfilling of Prophecies, observes, that when God intended to reveal any future events or high notions to his prophets, he then carried them either to the deserts, or the sea-shore, that having so separated them from amidst the press of people and business, and the cares of the world, he might settle their mind in a quiet repose, and there make them fit for revelation.

And this seems also to be imitated by the children of Israel, who having in a sad condition banished all mirth and musick from their pensive hearts, and having hung up their then mute harps upon the willow-trees growing by the rivers of Babylon, sat down upon those banks, bemoaning the ruins of Sion, and contemplating their own sad condition.

And an ingenious Spaniard says, that "rivers and the inhabitants of the watery element were made for wise men to contemplate, and fools to pass by without consideration." And though I will not rank myself in the number of the first, yet give me leave to free myself from the last, by offering to you a short contemplation, first of rivers, and then of fish; concerning which I doubt not but to give you many observations that will appear very considerable: I am sure they have appeared so to me, and made many an hour pass away more pleasantly, as I have sat quietly on a flowery bank by a calm river, and contemplated what I shall now relate to you.

And first concerning rivers; there be so many wonders reported and written of them, and of the several creatures that be bred and live in them, and those by authors of so good credit, that we need not to deny them an historical faith.

As namely of a river in Epirus that puts out any lighted torch, and kindles any torch that was not lighted. Some waters being drunk, cause madness, some drunkenness, and some laughter to death. The river Selarus in a few hours turns a rod or wand to stone: and our Camden mentions the like in England, and the like in Lochmere in Ireland. There is also a river in Arabia, of which all the sheep that drink thereof have their wool turned into a vermilion colour. And one of no less credit than Aristotle, tells us of a merry river, the river Elusina, that dances at the noise of musick, for with musick it bubbles, dances, and grows sandy, and so continues till the musick ceases, but then it presently returns to its wonted calmness and clearness. And Camden tells us of a well near to Kirby, in Westmoreland, that ebbs and flows several times every day: and he tells us of a river in Surrey, it is called Mole, that after it has run several miles, being opposed by hills, finds or makes itself a way under ground, and breaks out again so far off, that the inhabitants thereabout boast, as the Spaniards do of their river Anus, that they feed divers flocks of sheep upon a bridge. And lastly, for I would not tire your patience, one of no less authority than Josephus, that learned Jew, tells us of a river in Judea that runs swiftly all the six days of the week, and stands still and rests all their sabbath.

But I will lay aside my discourse of rivers, and tell you some things of the monsters, or fish, call them what you will, that they breed and feed in them. Pliny the philosopher says, in the third chapter of his ninth book, that in the Indian Sea, the fish called Balæna or Whirlpool, is so long and broad, as to take up more in length and breadth than two acres of ground; and, of other fish, of two hundred cubits long; and that in the river Ganges, there be Eels of thirty feet long. He says there, that these monsters appear in that sea, only when the tempestuous winds oppose the torrents of water falling from the rocks into it, and so turning what lay at the bottom to be seen on the water's top. And he says, that the people of Cadara, an island near this place, make the timber for their houses of those fish bones. He there tells us, that there are sometimes a thousand of these great Eels found wrapt or interwoven together. He tells us there, that it appears that dolphins love musick, and will come when called for, by some men or boys that know, and use to feed them; and that they can swim as swift as an arrow can be shot out of a bow; and much of this is spoken concerning the dolphin, and other fish, as may be found also in the learned Dr. Casaubon's *Discourse of Credulity and Incredulity*, printed by him about the year 1670.

I know, we Islanders are averse to the belief of these wonders; but there be so many strange creatures to be now seen, many collected by John Tradescant, and others added by my friend Elias Ashmole, Esq., who now keeps them carefully and methodically at his house near to Lambeth, near London, as may get some belief of some of the other wonders I mentioned. I will tell you some of the wonders that you may now see, and not till then believe, unless you think fit.

You may there see the Hog-fish, the Dog-fish, the Dolphin, the Cony-fish, the Parrot-fish, the Shark, the Poison-fish, Sword-fish, and not only other incredible fish, but you may there see the Salamander, several sorts of Barnacles, of Solan-Geese, the Bird of Paradise, such sorts of Snakes, and such Birds'-nests, and of so various forms, and so wonderfully made, as may beget wonder and amusement in any beholder; and so many hundred of other rarities in that collection, as will make the other wonders I spake of, the less incredible; for, you may note, that the waters are Nature's store-house, in which she locks up her wonders.

But, Sir, lest this discourse may seem tedious, I shall give it a sweet conclusion out of that holy poet, Mr. George Herbert his divine "Contemplation on God's Providence."

Lord! who hath praise enough, nay, who hath any?
None can express thy works, but he that knows them;
And none can know thy works, they are so many,
And so complete, but only he that owes them.

We all acknowledge both thy power and love
To be exact, transcendant, and divine;
Who dost so strangely and so sweetly move,
Whilst all things have their end, yet none but thine.

Wherefore, most sacred Spirit! I here present,
For me, and all my fellows, praise to thee;
And just it is, that I should pay the rent,
Because the benefit accrues to me.

And as concerning fish, in that psalm, wherein, for height of poetry and wonders, the prophet David seems even to exceed himself, how doth he there express himself in choice metaphors, even to the amazement of a contemplative reader, concerning the sea, the rivers, and the fish therein contained! And the great naturalist Pliny says, "That nature's great and wonderful power is more demonstrated in the sea than on the land." And this may appear, by the numerous and various creatures inhabiting both in and about that element; as to the readers of Gesner, Rondeletius, Pliny, Ausonius, Aristotle, and others, may be demonstrated. But I will sweeten this discourse also out of a contemplation in divine Du Bartas, who says:

God quickened in the sea, and in the rivers,
So many fishes of so many features,
That in the waters we may see all creatures,
Even all that on the earth are to be found,
As if the world were in deep waters drown'd.
For seas—as well as skies—have Sun, Moon, Stars;
As well as air—Swallows, Rooks, and Stares;
As well as earth—Vines, Roses, Nettles, Melons,
Mushrooms, Pinks, Gilliflowers, and many millions
Of other plants, more rare, more strange than these,
As very fishes, living in the seas;
As also Rams, Calves, Horses, Hares, and Hogs,
Wolves, Urchins, Lions, Elephants, and Dogs;
Yea, Men and Maids; and, which I most admire,
The mitred Bishop and the cowled Friar:
Of which, examples, but a few years since,
Were shewn the Norway and Polonian prince.

These seem to be wonders; but have had so many confirmations from men of learning and credit, that you need not doubt them. Nor are the number, nor the various shapes, of fishes more strange, or more fit for contemplation, than their different natures, inclinations, and actions; concerning which, I shall beg your patient ear a little longer.

The Cuttle-fish will cast a long gut out of her throat, which, like as an Angler doth his line, she sendeth forth, and pulleth in again at her pleasure, according as she sees some little fish come near to her; and the Cuttle-fish, being then hid in the gravel, lets the smaller fish nibble and bite the end of it; at which time she, by little and little, draws the smaller fish so near to her, that she may leap upon her, and then catches and devours her: and for this reason some have called this fish the Sea-angler.

And there is a fish called a Hermit, that at a certain age gets into a dead fish's shell, and, like a hermit, dwells there alone, studying the wind and weather; and so turns her shell, that she makes it defend her from the injuries that they would bring upon her.

There is also a fish called by Ælian the Adonis, or Darling of the Sea; so called, because it is a loving and innocent fish, a fish that hurts nothing that hath life, and is at peace with all the numerous inhabitants of that vast watery element; and truly, I think most Anglers are so disposed to most of mankind.

And there are, also, lustful and chaste fishes; of which I shall give you examples.

And first, what Du Bartas says of a fish called the Sargus; which, because none can express it better than he does, I shall give you in his own words, supposing it shall not have the less credit for being verse; for he hath gathered this and other observations out of authors that have been great and industrious searchers into the secrets of nature.

> The adult'rous Sargus doth not only change
> Wives every day, in the deep streams, but, strange!
> As if the honey of sea-love delight
> Could not suffice his ranging appetite,
> Goes courting she-goats on the grassy shore,
> Horning their husbands that had horns before.

And the same author writes concerning the Cantharus, that which you shall also hear in his own words:

> But, contrary, the constant Cantharus
> Is ever constant to his faithful spouse;
> In nuptial duties, spending his chaste life;
> Never loves any but his own dear wife.

Sir, but a little longer, and I have done.

VENATOR. Sir, take what liberty you think fit, for your discourse seems to be musick, and charms me to an attention.

PISCATOR. Why then, Sir, I will take a little liberty to tell, or rather to remember you what is said of Turtle-doves; first, that they silently plight their troth, and marry; and that then the survivor scorns, as the Thracian women are said to do, to outlive his or her mate; and this is taken for a truth; and if the survivor shall ever couple with another, then, not only the living, but the dead, be it either the he or the she, is denied the name and honour of a true Turtle-dove.

And to parallel this land-rarity, and teach mankind moral faithfulness, and to condemn those that talk of religion, and yet come short of the moral faith of fish and fowl, men that violate the law affirmed by St. Paul to be writ in their hearts, and which, he says, shall at the Last Day condemn and leave them without excuse—I pray hearken to what Du Bartas sings, for the hearing of such conjugal faithfulness will be musick to all chaste ears, and therefore I pray hearken to what Du Bartas sings of the Mullet.

> But for chaste love the Mullet hath no peer;
> For, if the fisher hath surpris'd her pheer,
> As mad with wo, to shore she followeth,
> Prest to consort him, both in life and death.

On the contrary, what shall I say of the House-Cock, which treads any hen; and, then, contrary to the Swan, the Partridge, and Pigeon, takes no care to hatch, to feed, or cherish his own brood, but is senseless, though they perish. And it is considerable, that the Hen, which, because she also takes any Cock, expects it not, who is sure the chickens be her own, hath by a moral impression her care and affection to her own brood more than doubled, even to such a height, that our Saviour, in expressing his love to Jerusalem, quotes her, for an example of tender affection, as his Father had done Job, for a pattern of patience.

And to parallel this Cock, there be divers fishes that cast their spawn on flags or stones, and then leave it uncovered, and exposed to become a prey and be devoured by vermin or other fishes. But other fishes, as namely the Barbel, take such care for the preservation of their seed, that, unlike to the Cock, or the Cuckoo, they mutually labour, both the spawner and the melter, to cover their spawn with sand, or watch it, or hide it in some secret place, unfrequented by vermin or by any fish but themselves.

Sir, these examples may, to you and others, seem strange; but they are testified, some by Aristotle, some by Pliny, some by Gesner, and by many others of credit; and are believed and known by divers, both of wisdom and experience, to be a truth; and indeed are, as I said at the beginning, fit for the contemplation of a most serious and a most pious man. And, doubtless, this made the prophet David say, "They that occupy themselves in deep waters, see the wonderful works of God": indeed such wonders, and pleasures too, as the land affords not.

And that they be fit for the contemplation of the most prudent, and pious, and peaceable men, seems to be testified by the practice of so many devout and contemplative men, as the Patriarchs and Prophets of old; and of the Apostles of our Saviour in our latter times, of which twelve, we are sure, he chose four that were simple fishermen, whom he inspired, and sent to publish his blessed will to the Gentiles; and inspired them also with a power to speak all languages, and by their powerful eloquence to beget faith in the unbelieving Jews; and themselves to suffer for that Saviour, whom their forefathers and they had crucified; and, in their sufferings, to preach freedom from the incumbrances of the law, and a new way to everlasting life: this was the employment of these happy fishermen. Concerning which choice, some have made these observations:

First, that he never reproved these, for their employment or calling, as he did the Scribes and the Money-changers. And secondly, he found that the hearts of such men, by nature, were fitted for contemplation and quietness; men of mild, and sweet, and peaceable spirits, as indeed most Anglers are: these men our blessed Saviour, who is observed to love to plant grace in good natures, though indeed nothing be too hard for him, yet these men he chose to call from their irreprovable employment of fishing, and gave them grace to be his disciples, and to follow him, and do wonders; I say four of twelve.

And it is observable, that it was our Saviour's will that these, our four fishermen, should have a priority of nomination in the catalogue of his twelve Apostles, as namely, first St. Peter, St. Andrew, St. James, and St. John; and, then, the rest in their order.

And it is yet more observable, that when our blessed Saviour went up into the mount, when he left the rest of his disciples, and chose only three to bear him company at his Transfiguration, that those three were all fishermen. And it is to be believed, that all the other Apostles, after they betook themselves to follow Christ, betook themselves to be fishermen too; for it is certain, that the greater number of them were found together, fishing, by Jesus after his resurrection, as it is recorded in the twenty-first chapter of St. John's gospel.

And since I have your promise to hear me with patience, I will take a liberty to look back upon an observation that hath been made by an ingenious and learned man; who observes, that God hath been pleased to allow those whom he himself hath appointed to write his holy will in holy writ, yet to express his will in such metaphors as their former affections or practice had inclined them to. And he brings Solomon for an example, who, before his conversion, was remarkably carnally amorous; and after, by God's appointment, wrote that spiritual dialogue, or holy amorous love-song the Canticles, betwixt God and his church: in which he says, "his beloved had eyes like the fish-pools of Heshbon."

And if this hold in reason, as I see none to the contrary, then it may be probably concluded, that Moses, who I told you before writ the book of Job, and the Prophet Amos, who was a shepherd, were both Anglers; for you shall, in all the Old Testament, find fish-hooks, I think but twice mentioned, namely, by meek Moses the friend of God, and by the humble prophet Amos.

Concerning which last, namely the prophet Amos, I shall make but this observation, that he that shall read the humble, lowly, plain style of that prophet, and compare it with the high, glorious, eloquent style of the prophet Isaiah, though they be both equally true, may easily believe Amos to be, not only a shepherd, but a good-natured plain fisherman. Which I do the rather believe, by comparing the affectionate, loving, lowly, humble Epistles of St. Peter, St. James, and St. John, whom we know were all fishers, with the glorious language and high metaphors of St. Paul, who we may believe was not.

And for the lawfulness of fishing: it may very well be maintained by our Saviour's bidding St. Peter cast his hook into the water and catch a fish, for money to pay tribute to Cæsar. And let me tell you, that Angling is of high esteem, and of much use in other nations. He that reads the Voyages of Ferdinand Mendez Pinto, shall find that there he declares to have found a king and several priests a-fishing. And he that reads Plutarch, shall find, that Angling was not contemptible in the days of Mark Antony and Cleopatra, and that they, in the midst of their wonderful glory, used Angling as a principal recreation. And let me tell you, that in the Scripture, Angling is always taken in the best sense; and that though hunting may be sometimes so taken, yet it is but seldom to be so understood. And let me add this more: he that views the ancient Ecclesiastical Canons, shall find hunting to be forbidden to Churchmen, as being a turbulent, toilsome, perplexing recreation; and shall find Angling allowed to clergymen, as being a harmless recreation, a recreation that invites them to contemplation and quietness.

I might here enlarge myself, by telling you what commendations our learned Perkins bestows on Angling: and how dear a lover, and great a practiser of it, our learned Dr. Whitaker was; as indeed many others of great learning have been. But I will content myself with two memorable men, that lived near to our own time, whom I also take to have been ornaments to the art of Angling.

The first is Dr. Nowel, sometime dean of the cathedral church of St. Paul, in London, where his monument stands yet undefaced; a man that, in the reformation of Queen Elizabeth, not that of Henry VIII., was so noted for his meek spirit, deep learning, prudence, and piety, that the then Parliament and Convocation, both, chose, enjoined, and trusted him to be the man to make a Catechism for public use, such a one as should stand as a rule for faith and manners to their posterity. And the good old man, though he was very learned, yet knowing that God leads us not to heaven by many, nor by hard questions, like an honest Angler, made that good, plain, unperplexed Catechism which is printed with our good old Service-book. I say, this good man was a dear lover and constant practiser of Angling, as any age can produce: and his custom was to spend besides his fixed hours of prayer, those hours which, by command of the church, were enjoined the clergy, and voluntarily dedicated to devotion by many primitive Christians, I say, besides those hours, this good man was observed to spend a tenth part of his time in Angling; and, also, for I have conversed with those which have conversed with him, to bestow a tenth part of his revenue, and usually all his fish, amongst the poor that inhabited near to those rivers in which it was caught; saying often, "that charity gave life to religion": and, at his return to his house, would praise God he had spent that day free from worldly trouble; both harmlessly, and in a recreation that became a churchman. And this good man was well content, if not desirous, that posterity should know he was an Angler; as may appear by his picture, now to be seen, and carefully kept, in Brazen-nose College, to which he was a liberal benefactor. In which picture he is drawn, leaning on a desk, with his Bible before him; and on one hand of him, his lines, hooks, and other tackling, lying in a round; and, on his other hand, are his Angle-rods of several sorts; and by them this is written, "that he died 13 Feb. 1601, being aged ninety-five years, forty-four of which he had been Dean of St. Paul's church; and that his age neither impaired his hearing, nor dimmed his eyes, nor weakened his memory, nor made any of the faculties of his mind weak or useless." It is said that Angling and temperance were great causes of these blessings; and I wish the like to all that imitate him, and love the memory of so good a man.

My next and last example shall be that under-valuer of money, the late provost of Eton College, Sir Henry Wotton, a man with whom I have often fished and conversed, a man whose foreign employments in the service of this nation, and whose experience, learning, wit, and cheerfulness, made his company to be esteemed one of the delights of mankind. This man, whose very approbation of Angling were sufficient to convince any modest censurer of it, this man was also a most dear lover, and a frequent practiser of the art of Angling; of which he would say, "it was an employment for his idle time, which was then not idly spent"; for Angling was, after tedious study, "a rest to his mind, a cheerer of his spirits, a diverter of sadness, a calmer of unquiet thoughts, a moderator of passions, a procurer of contentedness; and that it begat habits of peace and patience in those that professed and practiced it." Indeed, my friend, you will find Angling to be like the virtue of humility, which has a calmness of spirit, and a world of other blessings attending upon it.

Sir, this was the saying of that learned man. And I do easily believe, that peace, and patience, and a calm content, did cohabit in the cheerful heart of Sir Henry Wotton, because I know that when he was beyond seventy years of age, he made this description of a part of the present pleasure that possessed him, as he sat quietly, in a summer's evening, on a bank a-fishing. It is a description of the spring; which, because it glided as soft and sweetly from his pen, as that river does at this time, by which it was then made, I shall repeat it unto you:—

This day dame Nature seem'd in love;
The lusty sap began to move;
Fresh juice did stir th' embracing vines;
And birds had drawn their valentines.

The jealous trout, that low did lie,
Rose at a well-dissembled fly;
There stood my Friend, with patient skill,
Attending of his trembling quill.

Already were the eves possest
With the swift pilgrim's daubed nest;
The groves already did rejoice,
In Philomel's triumphing voice:

The showers were short, the weather mild,
The morning fresh, the evening smil'd.
Joan takes her neat-rubb'd pail, and now,
She trips to milk the sand-red cow;

Where, for some sturdy foot-ball swain,
Joan strokes a syllabub or twain.
The fields and gardens were beset
With tulips, crocus, violet;

And now, though late, the modest rose
Did more than half a blush disclose.
Thus all looks gay, and full of cheer,
To welcome the new-livery'd year.

These were the thoughts that then possessed the undisturbed mind of Sir Henry Wotton. Will you hear the wish of another Angler, and the commendation of his happy life, which he also sings in verse: *viz.* Jo. Davors, Esq.?

Let me live harmlessly, and near the brink
  Of Trent or Avon have a dwelling-place;
Where I may see my quill, or cork, down sink
  With eager bite of Perch, or Bleak, or Dace;
And on the world and my Creator think:
  Whilst some men strive ill-gotten goods t' embrace;

And others spend their time in base excess
Of wine, or worse, in war and wantonness.

Let them that list, these pastimes still pursue,
  And on such pleasing fancies feed their fill;
So I the fields and meadows green may view,
  And daily by fresh rivers walk at will,
Among the daisies and the violets blue,
  Red hyacinth, and yellow daffodil,
Purple Narcissus like the morning rays,
Pale gander-grass, and azure culver-keys.

I count it higher pleasure to behold
  The stately compass of the lofty sky;
And in the midst thereof, like burning gold,
  The flaming chariot of the world's great eye:
The watery clouds that in the air up-roll'd
  With sundry kinds of painted colours fly;
And fair Aurora, lifting up her head,
Still blushing, rise from old Tithonus' bed.

The hills and mountains raised from the plains,
  The plains extended level with the ground,
The grounds divided into sundry veins,
  The veins inclos'd with rivers running round;
These rivers making way through nature's chains,
  With headlong course, into the sea profound;
The raging sea, beneath the vallies low,
Where lakes, and rills, and rivulets do flow:

The lofty woods, the forests wide and long,
  Adorned with leaves and branches fresh and green,
In whose cool bowers the birds with many a song,
  Do welcome with their quire the summer's Queen;
The meadows fair, where Flora's gifts, among
  Are intermixt, with verdant grass between;
The silver-scaled fish that softly swim
Within the sweet brook's crystal, watery stream.

All these, and many more of his creation
  That made the heavens, the Angler oft doth see;
Taking therein no little delectation,
  To think how strange, how wonderful they be:
Framing thereof an inward contemplation
  To set his heart from other fancies free;
And whilst he looks on these with joyful eye,
His mind is rapt above the starry sky.

Sir, I am glad my memory has not lost these last verses, because they are somewhat more pleasant and more suitable to May-day than my harsh discourse. And I am glad your patience hath held out so long as to hear them and me, for both together have brought us within the sight of the Thatched House. And I must be your debtor, if you think it worth your attention, for the rest of my promised discourse, till some other opportunity, and a like time of leisure.

VENATOR. Sir, you have angled me on with much pleasure to the Thatched House; and I now find your words true, "that good company makes the way seem short"; for trust me, Sir, I thought we had wanted three miles of this house, till you showed it to me. But now we are at it, we'll turn into it, and refresh ourselves with a cup of drink, and a little rest.

PISCATOR. Most gladly, Sir, and we'll drink a civil cup to all the Otter-hunters that are to meet you to-morrow.

VENATOR. That we will, Sir, and to all the lovers of Angling too, of which number I am now willing to be one myself; for, by the help of your good discourse and company, I have put on new thoughts both of the art of Angling and of all that profess it; and if you will but meet me to-morrow at the time and place appointed, and bestow one day with me and my friends, in hunting the Otter, I will dedicate the next two days to wait upon you; and we too will, for that time, do nothing but angle, and talk of fish and fishing.

PISCATOR. It is a match, Sir, I will not fail you, God willing, to be at Amwell Hill to-morrow morning before sun-rising.

# THE SECOND DAY

## *On the Otter and the Chub*

### CHAPTER II

PISCATOR, VENATOR, HUNTSMAN, AND HOSTESS

VENATOR. My friend Piscator, you have kept time with my thoughts; for the sun is just rising, and I myself just now come to this place, and the dogs have just now put down an Otter. Look! down at the bottom of the hill there, in that meadow, chequered with water-lilies and lady-smocks; there you may see what work they make; look! look! you may see all busy; men and dogs; dogs and men; all busy.

PISCATOR. Sir, I am right glad to meet you, and glad to have so fair an entrance into this day's sport, and glad to see so many dogs, and more men, all in pursuit of the Otter. Let us compliment no longer, but join unto them. Come, honest Venator, let us be gone, let us make haste; I long to be doing; no reasonable hedge or ditch shall hold me.

VENATOR. Gentleman Huntsman, where found you this Otter?

HUNTSMAN. Marry, Sir, we found her a mile from this place, a-fishing. She has this morning eaten the greatest part of this Trout; she has only left thus much of it as you see, and was fishing for more; when we came we found her just at it: but we were here very early, we were here an hour before sunrise, and have given her no rest since we came; sure she will hardly escape all these dogs and men. I am to have the skin if we kill her.

VENATOR. Why, Sir, what is the skin worth?

HUNTSMAN. It is worth ten shillings to make gloves; the gloves of an Otter are the best fortification for your hands that can be thought on against wet weather.

PISCATOR. I pray, honest Huntsman, let me ask you a pleasant question: do you hunt a beast or a fish?

HUNTSMAN. Sir, it is not in my power to resolve you; I leave it to be resolved by the college of Carthusians, who have made vows never to eat flesh. But, I have heard, the question hath been debated among many great clerks, and they seem to differ about it; yet most agree that her tail is fish: and if her body be fish too, then I may say that a fish will walk upon land: for an Otter does so sometimes, five or six or ten miles in a night, to catch for her young ones, or to glut herself with fish. And I can tell you that Pigeons will fly forty miles for a breakfast: but, Sir, I am sure the Otter devours much fish, and kills and spoils much more than he eats. And I can tell you, that this dog-fisher, for so the Latins call him, can smell a fish in the water a hundred yards from him: Gesner says much farther: and that his stones are good against the falling sickness; and that there is an herb, Benione, which, being hung in a linen cloth near a fish-pond, or any haunt that he uses, makes him to avoid the place; which proves he smells both by water and land. And, I can tell you, there is brave hunting this water-dog in Cornwall; where there have been so many, that our learned Camden says there is a river called Ottersey, which was so named by reason of the abundance of Otters that bred and fed in it.

And thus much for my knowledge of the Otter; which you may now see above water at vent, and the dogs close with him; I now see he will not last long. Follow, therefore, my masters, follow; for Sweetlips was like to have him at this last vent.

VENATOR. Oh me! all the horse are got over the river, what shall we do now? shall we follow them over the water?

HUNTSMAN. No, Sir, no; be not so eager; stay a little, and follow me; for both they and the dogs will be suddenly on this side again, I warrant you, and the Otter too, it may be. Now have at him with Kilbuck, for he vents again.

VENATOR. Marry! so he does; for, look! he vents in that corner. Now, now, Ringwood has him: now, he is gone again, and has bit the poor dog. Now Sweetlips has her; hold her, Sweetlips! now all the dogs have her; some above and some under water: but, now, now she is tired, and past losing. Come bring her to me, Sweetlips. Look! it is a Bitch-otter, and she has lately whelp'd. Let's go to the place where she was put down; and, not far from it, you will find all her young ones, I dare warrant you, and kill them all too.

HUNTSMAN. Come, Gentlemen! come, all! let's go to the place where we put down the Otter. Look you! hereabout it was that she kennelled; look you! here it was indeed; for here's her young ones, no less than five: come, let us kill them all.

PISCATOR. No: I pray, Sir, save me one, and I'll try if I can make her tame, as I know an ingenious gentleman in Leicestershire, Mr. Nich. Segrave, has done; who hath not only made her tame, but to catch fish, and do many other things of much pleasure.

HUNTSMAN. Take one with all my heart; but let us kill the rest. And now let's go to an honest ale-house, where we may have a cup of good barley wine, and sing "Old Rose," and all of us rejoice together.

VENATOR. Come, my friend Piscator, let me invite you along with us. I'll bear your charges this night, and you shall bear mine to-morrow; for my intention is to accompany you a day or two in fishing.

PISCATOR. Sir, your request is granted; and I shall be right glad both to exchange such a courtesy, and also to enjoy your company.

## THE THIRD DAY

VENATOR. Well, now let's go to your sport of Angling.

PISCATOR. Let's be going, with all my heart. God keep you all, Gentlemen; and send you meet, this day, with another Bitch-otter, and kill her merrily, and all her young ones too.

VENATOR. Now, Piscator, where will you begin to fish?

PISCATOR. We are not yet come to a likely place; I must walk a mile further yet before I begin.

VENATOR. Well then, I pray, as we walk, tell me freely, how do you like your lodging, and mine host and the company? Is not mine host a witty man?

PISCATOR. Sir, I will tell you, presently, what I think of your host: but, first, I will tell you, I am glad these Otters were killed; and I am sorry there are no more Otter-killers; for I know that the want of Otter-killers, and the not keeping the fence-months for the preservation of fish, will, in time, prove the destruction of all rivers. And those very few that are left, that make conscience of the laws of the nation, and of keeping days of abstinence, will be forced to eat flesh, or suffer more inconveniences than are yet foreseen.

VENATOR. Why, Sir, what be those that you call the fence-months?

PISCATOR. Sir, they be principally three, namely, March, April, and May: for these be the usual months that Salmon come out of the sea to spawn in most fresh rivers. And their fry would, about a certain time, return back to the salt water, if they were not hindered by weirs and unlawful gins, which the greedy fishermen set, and so destroy them by thousands; as they would, being so taught by nature, change the fresh for salt water. He that shall view the wise Statutes made in the 13th of Edward the First, and the like in Richard the Second, may see several provisions made against the destruction of fish: and though I profess no knowledge of the law, yet I am sure the regulation of these defects might be easily mended. But I remember that a wise friend of mine did usually say, "that which is everybody's business is nobody's business": if it were otherwise, there could not be so many nets and fish, that are under the statute size, sold daily amongst us; and of which the conservators of the waters should be ashamed.

But, above all, the taking fish in spawning-time may be said to be against nature: it is like taking the dam on the nest when she hatches her young, a sin so against nature, that Almighty God hath in the Levitical law made a law against it.

But the poor fish have enemies enough besides such unnatural fishermen; as namely, the Otters that I spake of, the Cormorant, the Bittern, the Osprey, the Sea-gull, the Hern, the King-fisher, the Gorara, the Puet, the Swan, Goose, Duck, and the Craber, which some call the Water-rat: against all which any honest man may make a just quarrel, but I will not; I will leave them to be quarrelled with and killed by others, for I am not of a cruel nature, I love to kill nothing but fish.

And, now, to your question concerning your host. To speak truly, he is not to me a good companion, for most of his conceits were either scripture jests, or lascivious jests, for which I count no man witty: for the devil will help a man, that way inclined, to the first; and his own corrupt nature, which he always carries with him, to the latter. But a companion that feasts the company with wit and mirth, and leaves out the sin which is usually mixed with them, he is the man; and indeed such a companion should have his charges borne; and to such company I hope to bring you this night; for at Trout-hall, not far from this place, where I purpose to lodge to-night, there is usually an Angler that proves good company. And let me tell you, good company and good discourse are the very sinews of virtue. But for such discourse as we heard last night, it infects others: the very boys will learn to talk and swear, as they heard mine host, and another of the company that shall be nameless. I am sorry the other is a gentleman, for less religion will not save their souls than a beggar's: I think more will be required at the last great day. Well! you know what example is able to do; and I know what the poet says in the like case, which is worthy to be noted by all parents and people of civility:

> many a one
> Owes to his country his religion;
> And in another, would as strongly grow,
> Had but his nurse or mother taught him so.

This is reason put into verse, and worthy the consideration of a wise man. But of this no more; for though I love civility, yet I hate severe censures. I'll to my own art; and I doubt not but at yonder tree I shall catch a Chub: and then we'll turn to an honest cleanly hostess, that I know right well; rest ourselves there; and dress it for our dinner.

VENATOR. Oh, Sir! a Chub is the worst fish that swims; I hoped for a Trout to my dinner.

PISCATOR. Trust me, Sir, there is not a likely place for a Trout hereabout: and we staid so long to take our leave of your huntsmen this morning, that the sun is got so high, and shines so clear, that I will not undertake the catching of a Trout till evening. And though a Chub be, by you and many others, reckoned the worst of fish, yet you shall see I'll make it a good fish by dressing it.

VENATOR. Why, how will you dress him?

PISCATOR. I'll tell you by-and-by, when I have caught him. Look you here, Sir, do you see? but you must stand very close, there lie upon the top of the water, in this very hole, twenty Chubs. I'll catch only one and that shall be the biggest of them all: and that I will do so, I'll hold you twenty to one, and you shall see it done.

VENATOR. Ay, marry! Sir, now you talk like an artist; and I'll say you are one, when I shall see you perform what you say you can do: but I yet doubt it.

PISCATOR. You shall not doubt it long; for you shall see me do it presently. Look! the biggest of these Chubs has had some bruise upon his tail, by a Pike or some other accident; and that looks like a white spot. That very Chub I mean to put into your hands presently; sit you but down in the shade, and stay but a little while; and I'll warrant you, I'll bring him to you.

VENATOR. I'll sit down; and hope well, because you seem to be so confident.

PISCATOR. Look you, Sir, there is a trial of my skill; there he is: that very Chub, that I showed you, with the white spot on his tail. And I'll be as certain to make him a good dish of meat as I was to catch him: I'll now lead you to an honest ale-house, where we shall find a cleanly room, lavender in the windows, and twenty ballads stuck about the wall. There my hostess, which I may tell you is both cleanly, and handsome, and civil, hath dressed many a one for me; and shall now dress it after my fashion, and I warrant it good meat.

VENATOR. Come, Sir, with all my heart, for I begin to be hungry, and long to be at it, and indeed to rest myself too; for though I have walked but four miles this morning, yet I begin to be weary; yesterday's hunting hangs still upon me.

PISCATOR. Well, Sir, and you shall quickly be at rest, for yonder is the house I mean to bring you to.

Come, hostess, how do you? Will you first give us a cup of your best drink, and then dress this Chub, as you dressed my last, when I and my friend were here about eight or ten days ago? But you must do me one courtesy, it must be done instantly.

HOSTESS. I will do it, Mr. Piscator, and with all the speed I can.

PISCATOR. Now, Sir, has not my hostess made haste? and does not the fish look lovely?

VENATOR. Both, upon my word, Sir; and therefore let's say grace and fall to eating of it.

PISCATOR. Well, Sir, how do you like it?

VENATOR. Trust me, 'tis as good meat as I ever tasted. Now let me thank you for it, drink to you and beg a courtesy of you; but it must not be denied me.

PISCATOR. What is it, I pray, Sir? You are so modest, that methinks I may promise to grant it before it is asked.

VENATOR. Why, Sir, it is, that from henceforth you would allow me to call you Master, and that really I may be your scholar; for you are such a companion, and have so quickly caught and so excellently cooked this fish, as makes me ambitious to be your scholar.

PISCATOR. Give me your hand; from this time forward I will be your Master, and teach you as much of this art as I am able; and will, as you desire me, tell you somewhat of the nature of most of the fish that we are to angle for, and I am sure I both can and will tell you more than any common angler yet knows.

# THE THIRD DAY—*continued*

## *How to fish for, and to dress, the Chavender or Chub*

### CHAPTER III

#### PISCATOR AND VENATOR

PISCATOR. The Chub, though he eat well, thus dressed, yet as he is usually dressed, he does not. He is objected against, not only for being full of small forked bones, dispersed through all his body, but that he eats waterish, and that the flesh of him is not firm, but short and tasteless. The French esteem him so mean, as to call him *Un Villain*; nevertheless he may be so dressed as to make him very good meat; as, namely, if he be a large Chub, then dress him thus:

First, scale him, and then wash him clean, and then take out his guts; and to that end make the hole as little, and near to his gills, as you may conveniently, and especially make clean his throat from the grass and weeds that are usually in it; for if that be not very clean, it will make him to taste very sour. Having so done, put some sweet herbs into his belly; and then tie him with two or three splinters to a spit, and roast him, basted often with vinegar, or rather verjuice and butter, with good store of salt mixed with it.

Being thus dressed, you will find him a much better dish of meat than you, or most folk, even than anglers themselves, do imagine: for this dries up the fluid watery humour with which all Chubs do abound. But take this rule with you, That a Chub newly taken and newly dressed, is so much better than a Chub of a day's keeping after he is dead, that I can compare him to nothing so fitly as to cherries newly gathered from a tree, and others that have been bruised and lain a day or two in water. But the Chub being thus used, and dressed presently; and not washed after he is gutted, for note, that lying long in water, and washing the blood out of any fish after they be gutted, abates much of their sweetness; you will find the Chub, being dressed in the blood, and quickly, to be such meat as will recompense your labour, and disabuse your opinion.

Or you may dress the Chavender or Chub thus:

When you have scaled him, and cut off his tail and fins, and washed him very clean, then chine or slit him through the middle, as a salt-fish is usually cut; then give him three or four cuts or scotches on the back with your knife, and broil him on charcoal, or wood coal, that are free from smoke; and all the time he is a-broiling, baste him with the best sweet butter, and good store of salt mixed with it. And, to this, add a little thyme cut exceedingly small, or bruised into the butter. The Cheven thus dressed hath the watery taste taken away, for which so many except against him. Thus was the Cheven dressed that you now liked so well, and commended so much. But note again, that if this Chub that you eat of had been kept till to-morrow, he had not been worth a rush. And remember, that his throat be washed very clean, I say very clean, and his body not washed after he is gutted, as indeed no fish should be.

Well, scholar, you see what pains I have taken to recover the lost credit of the poor despised Chub. And now I will give you some rules how to catch him: and I am glad to enter you into the art of fishing by catching a Chub, for there is no fish better to enter a young Angler, he is so easily caught, but then it must be this particular way:

Go to the same hole in which I caught my Chub, where, in most hot days, you will find a dozen or twenty Chevens floating near the top of the water. Get two or three grasshoppers, as you go over the meadow: and get secretly behind the tree, and stand as free from motion as is possible. Then put a grasshopper on your hook, and let your hook hang a quarter of a yard short of the water, to which end you must rest your rod on some bough of the tree. But it is likely the Chubs will sink down towards the bottom of the water, at the first shadow of your rod (for Chub is the fearfullest of fishes), and will do so if but a bird flies over him and makes the least shadow on the water; but they will presently rise up to the top again, and there lie soaring till some shadow affrights them again. I say, when they lie upon the top of the water, look out the best Chub, which you, setting yourself in a fit place, may very easily see, and move your rod, as softly as a snail moves, to that Chub you intend to catch; let your bait fall gently upon the water three or four inches before him, and he will infallibly take the bait. And you will be as sure to catch him; for he is one of the leather-mouthed fishes, of which a hook does scarce ever lose its hold; and therefore give him play enough before you offer to take him out of the water. Go your way presently; take my rod, and do as I bid you; and I will sit down and mend my tackling till you return back.

VENATOR. Truly, my loving master, you have offered me as fair as I could wish. I'll go and observe your directions.

Look you, master, what I have done, that which joys my heart, caught just such another Chub as yours was.

PISCATOR. Marry, and I am glad of it: I am like to have a towardly scholar of you. I now see, that with advice and practice, you will make an Angler in a short time. Have but a love to it; and I'll warrant you.

VENATOR. But, master! what if I could not have found a grasshopper?

PISCATOR. Then I may tell you, That a black snail, with his belly slit, to show his white, or a piece of soft cheese, will usually do as well. Nay, sometimes a worm, or any kind of fly, as the ant-fly, the flesh-fly, or wall-fly; or the dor or beetle, which you may find under cow-dung; or a bob, which you will find in the same place, and in time will be a beetle; it is a short white worm, like to and bigger than a gentle; or a cod-worm; or a case-worm; any of these will do very well to fish in such a manner.

And after this manner you may catch a Trout in a hot evening: when, as you walk by a brook, and shall see or hear him leap at flies, then, if you get a grasshopper, put it on your hook, with your line about two yards long; standing behind a bush or tree where his hole is: and make your bait stir up and down on the top of the water. You may, if you stand close, be sure of a bite, but not sure to catch him, for he is not a leather-mouthed fish. And after this manner you may fish for him with almost any kind of live fly, but especially with a grasshopper.

VENATOR. But before you go further, I pray, good master, what mean you by a leather-mouthed fish?

PISCATOR. By a leather-mouthed fish, I mean such as have their teeth in their throat, as the Chub or Cheven: and so the Barbel, the Gudgeon, and Carp, and divers others have. And the hook being stuck into the leather, or skin, of the mouth of such fish, does very seldom or never lose its hold: but on the contrary, a Pike, a Perch, or Trout, and so some other fish, which have not their teeth in their throats, but in their mouths, which you shall observe to be very full of bones, and the skin very thin, and little of it. I say, of these fish the hook never takes so sure hold but you often lose your fish, unless he have gorged it.

VENATOR. I thank you, good master, for this observation. But now what shall be done with my Chub or Cheven that I have caught?

PISCATOR. Marry, Sir, it shall be given away to some poor body; for I'll warrant you I'll give you a Trout for your supper: and it is a good beginning of your art to offer your first-fruits to the poor, who will both thank you and God for it, which I see by your silence you seem to consent to. And for your willingness to part with it so charitably, I will also teach more concerning Chub-fishing. You are to note, that in March and April he is usually taken with worms; in May, June, and July, he will bite at any fly, or at cherries, or at beetles with their legs and wings cut off, or at any kind of snail, or at the black bee that breeds in clay walls. And he never refuses a grasshopper, on the top of a swift stream, nor, at the bottom, the young humble bee that breeds in long grass, and is ordinarily found by the mower of it. In August, and in the cooler months, a yellow paste, made of the strongest cheese, and pounded in a mortar, with a little butter and saffron, so much of it as, being beaten small, will turn it to a lemon colour. And some make a paste for the winter months, at which time the Chub is accounted best, for then it is observed, that the forked bones are lost, or turned into a kind of gristle, especially if he be baked, of cheese and turpentine. He will bite also at a minnow, or penk, as a Trout will: of which I shall tell you more hereafter, and of divers other baits. But take this for a rule, that, in hot weather, he is to be fished for towards the mid-water, or near the top; and in colder weather, nearer the bottom; and if you fish for him on the top, with a beetle, or any fly, then be sure to let your line be very long, and to keep out of sight. And having told you, that his spawn is excellent meat, and that the head of a large Cheven, the throat being well washed, is the best part of him, I will say no more of this fish at the present, but wish you may catch the next you fish for.

But, lest you may judge me too nice in urging to have the Chub dressed so presently after he is taken, I will commend to your consideration how curious former times have been in the like kind.

You shall read in Seneca, his *Natural Questions*, that the ancients were so curious in the newness of their fish, that that semed not new enough that was not put alive into the guest's hand; and he says, that to that end they did usually keep them living in glass bottles in their dining-rooms, and they did glory much in their entertaining of friends, to have that fish taken from under their table alive that was instantly to be fed upon; and he says, they took great pleasure to see their Mullets change to several colours when they were dying. But enough of this; for I doubt I have staid too long from giving you some Observations of the Trout, and how to fish for him, which shall take up the next of my spare time.

## THE THIRD DAY—*continued*

*On the Nature and Breeding of the Trout, and how to fish for him*

### CHAPTER IV

PISCATOR, VENATOR, MILK-WOMAN, MAUDLIN, HOSTESS

PISCATOR. The Trout is a fish highly valued, both in this and foreign nations. He may be justly said, as the old poet said of wine, and we English say of venison, to be a generous fish: a fish that is so like the buck, that he also has his seasons; for it is observed, that he comes in and goes out of season with the stag and buck. Gesner says, his name is of a German offspring; and says he is a fish that feeds clean and purely, in the swiftest streams, and on the hardest gravel; and that he may justly contend with all fresh water fish, as the Mullet may with all sea fish, for precedency and daintiness of taste; and that being in right season, the most dainty palates have allowed precedency to him.

And before I go farther in my discourse, let me tell you, that you are to observe, that as there be some barren does that are good in summer, so there be some barren Trouts that are good in winter; but there are not many that are so; for usually they be in their perfection in the month of May, and decline with the buck. Now you are to take notice, that in several countries, as in Germany, and in other parts, compared to ours, fish do differ much in their bigness, and shape, and other ways; and so do Trouts. It is well known that in the Lake Leman, the Lake of Geneva, there are Trouts taken of three cubits long; as is affirmed by Gesner, a writer of good credit: and Mercator says, the Trouts that are taken in the Lake of Geneva are a great part of the merchandize of that famous city. And you are further to know, that there be certain waters that breed Trouts remarkable, both for their number and smallness. I know a little brook in Kent, that breeds them to a number incredible, and you may take them twenty or forty in an hour, but none greater than about the size of a Gudgeon. There are also, in divers rivers, especially that relate to, or be near to the sea, as Winchester, or the Thames about Windsor, a little Trout called a Samlet, or Skegger

Trout, in both which places I have caught twenty or forty at a standing, that will bite as fast and as freely as Minnows: these be by some taken to be young Salmons; but in those waters they never grow to be bigger than a Herring.

There is also in Kent, near to Canterbury, a Trout called there a Fordidge Trout, a Trout that bears the name of the town where it is usually caught, that is accounted the rarest of fish; many of them near the bigness of a Salmon, but known by their different colour; and in their best season they cut very white: and none of these have been known to be caught with an angle, unless it were one that was caught by Sir George Hastings, an excellent angler, and now with God: and he hath told me, he thought that Trout bit not for hunger but wantonness; and it is the rather to be believed, because both he, then, and many others before him, have been curious to search into their bellies, what the food was by which they lived; and have found out nothing by which they might satisfy their curiosity.

Concerning which you are to take notice, that it is reported by good authors, that grasshoppers and some fish have no mouths, but are nourished and take breath by the porousness of their gills, man knows not how: and this may be believed, if we consider that when the raven hath hatched her eggs, she takes no further care, but leaves her young ones to the care of the God of nature, who is said, in the Psalms, "to feed the young ravens that call upon him." And they be kept alive and fed by a dew; or worms that breed in their nests; or some other ways that we mortals know not. And this may be believed of the Fordidge Trout, which, as it is said of the stork, that he knows his season, so he knows his times, I think almost his day of coming into that river out of the sea; where he lives, and, it is like, feeds, nine months of the year, and fasts three in the river of Fordidge. And you are to note, that those townsmen are very punctual in observing the time of beginning to fish for them; and boast much, that their river affords a Trout that exceeds all others. And just so does Sussex boast of several fish; as, namely, a Shelsey Cockle, a Chichester Lobster, an Arundel Mullet, and an Amerly Trout.

And, now, for some confirmation of the Fordidge Trout: you are to know that this Trout is thought to eat nothing in the fresh water; and it may be the better believed, because it is well known, that swallows, and bats, and wagtails, which are called half-year birds, and not seen to fly in England for six months in the year, but about Michaelmas leave us for a hotter climate, yet some of them that have been left behind their fellows, have been found, many thousands at a time, in hollow trees, or clay caves, where they have been observed to live, and sleep out the whole winter, without meat. And so Albertus observes, That there is one kind of frog that hath her mouth naturally shut up about the end of August, and that she lives so all the winter: and though it be strange to some, yet it is known to too many among us to be doubted.

And so much for these Fordidge Trouts, which never afford an angler sport, but either live their time of being in the fresh water, by their meat formerly gotten in the sea, not unlike the swallow or frog, or, by the virtue of the fresh water only; or, as the birds of Paradise and the cameleon are said to live, by the sun and the air.

There is also in Northumberland a Trout called a Bull-trout, of a much greater length and bigness than any in these southern parts; and there are, in many rivers that relate to the sea, Salmon-trouts, as much different from others, both in shape and in their spots, as we see sheep in some countries differ one from another in their shape and bigness, and in the fineness of the wool: and, certainly, as some pastures breed larger sheep; so do some rivers, by reason of the ground over which they run, breed larger Trouts.

Now the next thing that I will commend to your consideration is, that the Trout is of a more sudden growth than other fish. Concerning which, you are also to take notice, that he lives not so long as the Pearch, and divers other fishes do, as Sir Francis Bacon hath observed in his History of Life and Death.

And next you are to take notice, that he is not like the Crocodile, which if he lives never so long, yet always thrives till his death: but 'tis not so with the Trout; for after he is come to his full growth, he declines in his body, and keeps his bigness, or thrives only in his head till his death. And you are to know, that he will, about, especially before, the time of his spawning, get, almost miraculously, through weirs and flood-gates, against the stream; even through such high and swift places as is almost incredible. Next, that the Trout usually spawns about October or November, but in some rivers a little sooner or later; which is the more observable, because most other fish spawn in the spring or summer, when the sun hath warmed both the earth and water, and made it fit for generation. And you are to note, that he continues many months out of season; for it may be observed of the Trout, that he is like the Buck or the Ox, that will not be fat in many months, though he go in the very same pastures that horses do, which will be fat in one month: and so you may observe, That most other fishes recover strength, and grow sooner fat and in season than the Trout doth.

And next you are to note, That till the sun gets to such a height as to warm the earth and the water, the Trout is sick, and lean, and lousy, and unwholesome; for you shall, in winter, find him to have a big head, and, then, to be lank and thin and lean; at which time many of them have sticking on them Sugs, or Trout-lice; which is a kind of a worm, in shape like a clove, or pin with a big head, and sticks close to him, and sucks his moisture; those, I think, the Trout breeds himself: and never thrives till he free himself from them, which is when warm weather comes; and, then, as he grows stronger, he gets from the dead still water into the sharp streams and the gravel, and, there, rubs off these worms or lice; and then, as he grows stronger, so he gets him into swifter and swifter streams, and there lies at the watch for any fly or minnow that comes near to him; and he especially loves the May-fly, which is bred of the cod-worm, or cadis; and these make the Trout bold and lusty, and he is usually fatter and better meat at the end of that month than at any time of the year.

Now you are to know that it is observed, that usually the best Trouts are either red or yellow; though some, as the Fordidge Trout, be white and yet good; but that is not usual: and it is a note observable, that the female Trout hath usually a less head, and a deeper body than the male Trout, and is usually the better meat. And note, that a hog back and a little head, to either Trout, Salmon or any other fish, is a sign that that fish is in season.

But yet you are to note, that as you see some willows or palm-trees bud and blossom sooner than others do, so some Trouts be, in rivers, sooner in season: and as some hollies, or oaks, are longer before they cast their leaves, so are some Trouts, in rivers, longer before they go out of season.

And you are to note, that there are several kinds of Trouts: but these several kinds are not considered but by very few men; for they go under the general name of Trouts; just as pigeons do, in most places; though it is certain, there are tame and wild pigeons; and of the tame, there be helmits and runts, and carriers and cropers, and indeed too many to name. Nay, the Royal Society have found and published lately, that there be thirty and three kinds of spiders; and yet all, for aught I know, go under that one general name of spider. And it is so with many kinds of fish, and of Trouts especially; which differ in their bigness, and shape, and spots, and colour. The great Kentish hens may be an instance, compared to other hens: and, doubtless, there is a kind of small Trout, which will never thrive to be big; that breeds very many more than others do, that be of a larger size: which you may rather believe, if you consider that the little wren and titmouse will have twenty young ones at a time, when, usually, the noble hawk, or the musical thrassel or blackbird, exceed not four or five.

And now you shall see me try my skill to catch a Trout; and at my next walking, either this evening or to-morrow morning, I will give you direction how you yourself shall fish for him.

VENATOR. Trust me, master, I see now it is a harder matter to catch a Trout than a Chub; for I have put on patience, and followed you these two hours, and not seen a fish stir, neither at your minnow nor your worm.

PISCATOR. Well, scholar, you must endure worse luck sometime, or you will never make a good angler. But what say you now? there is a Trout now, and a good one too, if I can but hold him; and two or three turns more will tire him. Now you see he lies still, and the sleight is to land him: reach me that landing-net. So, Sir, now he is mine own: what say you now, is not this worth all my labour and your patience?

VENATOR. On my word, master, this is a gallant Trout; what shall we do with him?

PISCATOR. Marry, e'en eat him to supper: we'll go to my hostess from whence we came; she told me, as I was going out of door, that my brother Peter, a good angler and a cheerful companion, had sent word he would lodge there to-night, and bring a friend with him. My hostess has two beds, and I know you and I may have the best: we'll rejoice with my brother Peter and his friend, tell tales, or sing ballads, or make a catch, or find some harmless sport to content us, and pass away a little time without offence to God or man.

VENATOR. A match, good master, let's go to that house, for the linen looks white, and smells of lavender, and I long to lie in a pair of sheets that smell so. Let's be going, good master, for I am hungry again with fishing.

PISCATOR. Nay, stay a little, good scholar. I caught my last Trout with a worm; now I will put on a minnow, and try a quarter of an hour about yonder trees for another; and, so, walk towards our lodging. Look you, scholar, thereabout we shall have a bite presently, or not at all. Have with you, Sir: o' my word I have hold of him. Oh! it is a great logger-headed Chub; come, hang him upon that willow twig, and let's be going. But turn out of the way a little, good scholar! toward yonder high honeysuckle hedge; there we'll sit and sing, whilst this shower falls so gently upon the teeming earth, and gives yet a sweeter smell to the lovely flowers that adorn these verdant meadows.

Look! under that broad beech-tree I sat down, when I was last this way a-fishing; and the birds in the adjoining grove seemed to have a friendly contention with an echo, whose dead voice seemed to live in a hollow tree near to the brow of that primrose-hill. There I sat viewing the silver streams glide silently towards their centre, the tempestuous sea; yet sometimes opposed by rugged roots and pebble-stones, which broke their waves, and turned them into foam; and sometimes I beguiled time by viewing the harmless lambs; some leaping securely in the cool shade, whilst others sported themselves in the cheerful sun; and saw others craving comfort from the swollen udders of their bleating dams. As I thus sat, these and other sights had so fully possest my soul with content, that I thought, as the poet has happily exprest it,

> I was for that time lifted above earth;
> And possest joys not promis'd in my birth.

As I left this place, and entered into the next field, a second pleasure entertained me; 'twas a handsome milk-maid, that had not yet attained so much age and wisdom as to load her mind with any fears of many things that will never be, as too many men too often do; but she cast away all care, and sung like a nightingale. Her voice was good, and the ditty fitted for it; it was that smooth song which was made by Kit Marlow, now at least fifty years ago; and the milk-maid's mother sung an answer to it, which was made by Sir Walter Raleigh, in his younger days. They were old-fashioned poetry, but choicely good; I think much better than the strong lines that are now in fashion in this critical age. Look yonder! on my word, yonder, they both be a-milking again. I will give her the Chub, and persuade them to sing those two songs to us.

God speed you, good woman! I have been a-fishing; and am going to Bleak Hall to my bed; and having caught more fish than will sup myself and my friend, I will bestow this upon you and your daughter, for I use to sell none.

MILK-WOMAN. Marry! God requite you, Sir, and we'll eat it cheerfully. And if you come this way a-fishing two months hence, a grace of God! I'll give you a syllabub of new verjuice, in a new-made hay-cock, for it. And my Maudlin shall sing you one of her best ballads; for she and I both love all anglers, they be such honest, civil, quiet men. In the meantime will you drink a draught of red cow's milk? you shall have it freely.

PISCATOR. No, I thank you; but, I pray, do us a courtesy that shall stand you and your daughter in nothing, and yet we will think ourselves still something in your debt: it is but to sing us a song that was sung by your daughter when I last passed over this meadow, about eight or nine days since.

MILK-WOMAN. What song was it, I pray? Was it, "Come, Shepherds, deck your herds"? or, "As at noon Dulcina rested"? or, "Phillida flouts me"? or, "Chevy Chace"? or, "Johnny Armstrong"? or, "Troy Town"?

PISCATOR. No, it is none of those; it is a Song that your daughter sung the first part, and you sung the answer to it.

MILK-WOMAN. O, I know it now. I learned the first part in my golden age, when I was about the age of my poor daughter; and the latter part, which indeed fits me best now, but two or three years ago, when the cares of the world began to take hold of me: but you shall, God willing, hear them both; and sung as well as we can, for we both love anglers.

Come, Maudlin, sing the first part to the gentlemen, with a merry heart; and I'll sing the second when you have done.

THE MILK-MAID'S SONG.

Come, live with me, and be my love,
And we will all the pleasures prove,
That valleys, groves, or hills, or fields,
Or woods, and steepy mountains yields;

Where we will sit upon the rocks,
And see the shepherds feed our flocks,
By shallow rivers, to whose falls
Melodious birds sing madrigals.

And I will make thee beds of roses;
And, then, a thousand fragrant posies;
A cap of flowers, and a kirtle,
Embroidered all with leaves of myrtle;

A gown made of the finest wool,
Which from our pretty lambs we pull;
Slippers, lin'd choicely for the cold,
With buckles of the purest gold;

A belt of straw and ivy-buds,
With coral clasps, and amber studs.
And if these pleasures may thee move,
Come, live with me, and be my love.

Thy silver dishes, for thy meat,
As precious as the Gods do eat,
Shall, on an ivory table, be
Prepared each day for thee and me.

The shepherd swains shall dance and sing
For thy delight, each May morning.
If these delights thy mind may move,
Then live with me, and be my love.

VENATOR. Trust me, master, it is a choice song, and sweetly sung by honest Maudlin. I now see it was not without cause that our good queen Elizabeth did so often wish herself a milk-maid all the month of May, because they are not troubled with fears and cares, but sing sweetly all the day, and sleep securely all the night: and without doubt, honest, innocent, pretty Maudlin does so. I'll bestow Sir Thomas Overbury's milk-maid's wish upon her, "that she may die in the Spring; and, being dead, may have good store of flowers stuck round about her winding-sheet."

THE MILK-MAID'S MOTHER'S ANSWER

If all the world and love were young,
And truth in every shepherd's tongue,
These pretty pleasures might me move
To live with thee, and be thy love.

But Time drives flocks from field to fold;
When rivers rage, and rocks grow cold;
Then Philomel becometh dumb;
And age complains of cares to come.

The flowers do fade, and wanton fields
To wayward winter reckoning yields.
A honey tongue, a heart of gall,
Is fancy's spring but sorrow's fall.

Thy gowns, thy shoes, thy beds of roses,
Thy cap, thy kirtle, and thy posies,
Soon break, soon wither, soon forgotten;
In folly ripe, in reason rotten.

Thy belt of straw, and ivy buds,
Thy coral clasps, and amber studs,
All these in me no means can move
To come to thee, and be thy love.

What should we talk of dainties, then,
Of better meat than's fit for men?
These are but vain: that's only good
Which God hath blessed, and sent for food.

But could youth last, and love still breed;
Had joys no date, nor age no need;
Then those delights my mind might move
To live with thee, and be thy love.

MOTHER. Well! I have done my song. But stay, honest anglers; for I will make Maudlin sing you one short song more. Maudlin! sing that song that you sung last night, when young Coridon the shepherd played so purely on his oaten pipe to you and your cousin Betty.

MAUDLIN. I will, mother.

I married a wife of late,
The more's my unhappy fate:
I married her for love,
As my fancy did me move,
And not for a worldly estate:

But oh! the green sickness
Soon changed her likeness;

And all her beauty did fail.
But 'tis not so
With those that go
Thro' frost and snow
As all men know,
And carry the milking-pail.

PISCATOR. Well sung, good woman; I thank you. I'll give you another dish of fish one of these days; and then beg another song of you. Come, scholar! let Maudlin alone: do not you offer to spoil her voice. Look! yonder comes mine hostess, to call us to supper. How now! is my brother Peter come?

HOSTESS. Yes, and a friend with him. They are both glad to hear that you are in these parts; and long to see you; and long to be at supper, for they be very hungry.

## THE THIRD DAY—*continued*

### *On the Trout*

### CHAPTER V

PISCATOR, PETER, VENATOR, CORIDON

PISCATOR. Well met, brother Peter! I heard you and a friend would lodge here to-night; and that hath made me to bring my friend to lodge here too. My friend is one that would fain be a brother of the angle: he hath been an angler but this day; and I have taught him how to catch a Chub, by dapping with a grasshopper; and the Chub he caught was a lusty one of nineteen inches long. But pray, brother Peter, who is your companion?

PETER. Brother Piscator, my friend is an honest countryman, and his name is Coridon; and he is a downright witty companion, that met me here purposely to be pleasant and eat a Trout; and I have not yet wetted my line since we met together: but I hope to fit him with a Trout for his breakfast; for I'll be early up.

PISCATOR. Nay, brother, you shall not stay so long; for, look you! here is a Trout will fill six reasonable bellies.

Come, hostess, dress it presently; and get us what other meat the house will afford; and give us some of your best barley-wine, the good liquor that our honest forefathers did use to think of; the drink which preserved their health, and made them live so long, and to do so many good deeds.

PETER. On my word, this Trout is perfect in season. Come, I thank you, and here is a hearty draught to you, and to all the brothers of the angle wheresoever they be, and to my young brother's good fortune tomorrow. I will furnish him with a rod, if you will furnish him with the rest of the tackling: we will set him up, and make him a fisher. And I will tell him one thing for his encouragement, that his fortune hath made him happy to be scholar to such a master; a master that knows as much, both of the nature and breeding of fish, as any man; and can also tell him as well how to catch and cook them, from the Minnow to the Salmon, as any that I ever met withal.

PISCATOR. Trust me, brother Peter, I find my scholar to be so suitable to my own humour, which is to be free and pleasant and civilly merry, that my resolution is to hide nothing that I know from him. Believe me, scholar, this is my resolution; and so here's to you a hearty draught, and to all that love us and the honest art of Angling.

VENATOR. Trust me, good master, you shall not sow your seed in barren ground; for I hope to return you an increase answerable to your hopes: but, however, you shall find me obedient, and thankful, and serviceable to my best ability.

PISCATOR. 'Tis enough, honest scholar! come, let's to supper. Come, my friend Coridon, this Trout looks lovely; it was twenty-two inches when it was taken; and the belly of it looked, some part of it, as yellow as a marigold, and part of it as white as a lily; and yet, methinks, it looks better in this good sauce.

CORIDON. Indeed, honest friend, it looks well, and tastes well: I thank you for it, and so doth my friend Peter, or else he is to blame.

PETER. Yes, and so I do; we all thank you: and, when we have supped, I will get my friend Coridon to sing you a song for requital.

CORIDON. I will sing a song, if anybody will sing another, else, to be plain with you, I will sing none. I am none of those that sing for meat, but for company: I say,

"'Tis merry in hall,
When men sing all."

PISCATOR. I'll promise you I'll sing a song that was lately made, at my request, by Mr. William Basse; one that hath made the choice songs of the "Hunter in his Career," and of "Tom of Bedlam," and many others of note; and this, that I will sing, is in praise of Angling.

CORIDON. And then mine shall be the praise of a Countryman's life. What will the rest sing of?

PETER. I will promise you, I will sing another song in praise of Angling to-morrow night; for we will not part till then; but fish to-morrow, and sup together: and the next day every man leave fishing, and fall to his business.

VENATOR. 'Tis a match; and I will provide you a song or a catch against then, too, which shall give some addition of mirth to the company; for we will be civil and as merry as beggars.

PISCATOR. 'Tis a match, my masters. Let's e'en say grace, and turn to the fire, drink the other cup to whet our whistles, and so sing away all sad thoughts. Come on, my masters, who begins? I think it is best to draw cuts, and avoid contention.

PETER. It is a match. Look, the shortest cut falls to Coridon.

CORIDON. Well, then, I will begin, for I hate contention.

CORIDON'S SONG.

Oh the sweet contentment
The countryman doth find!
    Heigh trolollie lollie loe,
    Heigh trolollie lee.
That quiet contemplation
Possesseth all my mind:
    Then care away,
    And wend along with me.

For Courts are full of flattery,
As hath too oft been tried;
    Heigh trolollie lollie loe, etc.
The city full of wantonness,
And both are full of pride:
    Then care away, etc.

But oh, the honest countryman
Speaks truly from his heart,
    Heigh trolollie lollie loe, etc.
His pride is in his tillage,
His horses, and his cart:
    Then care away, etc.

Our cloathing is good sheep-skins,
Grey russet for our wives;
    Heigh trolollie lollie loe, etc.
'Tis warmth and not gay cloathing
That doth prolong our lives:
    Then care away, etc.

The ploughman, tho' he labour hard,
Yet on the holy-day,
    Heigh trolollie lollie loe, etc.
No emperor so merrily
Does pass his time away:
    Then care away, etc.

To recompense our tillage,
The heavens afford us showers;
    Heigh trolollie lollie loe, etc.
And for our sweet refreshments
The earth affords us bowers:
    Then care away, etc.

The cuckow and the nightingale
Full merrily do sing,
    Heigh trolollie lollie loe, etc.
And with their pleasant roundelays

Bid welcome to the spring:
    Then care away, etc.

This is not half the happiness
The countryman enjoys;
    Heigh trolollie lollie loe, etc.
Though others think they have as much,
Yet he that says so lies:
    Then come away,
    Turn countrymen with me.

JO. CHALKHILL.

PISCATOR. Well sung, Coridon, this song was sung with mettle; and it was choicely fitted to the occasion: I shall love you for it as long as I know you. I would you were a brother of the angle; for a companion that is cheerful, and free from swearing and scurrilous discourse, is worth gold. I love such mirth as does not make friends ashamed to look upon one another next morning; nor men, that cannot well bear it, to repent the money they spend when they be warmed with drink. And take this for a rule: you may pick out such times and such companies, that you make yourselves merrier for a little than a great deal of money; for "'Tis the company and not the charge that makes the feast"; and such a companion you prove: I thank you for it.

But I will not compliment you out of the debt that I owe you, and therefore I will begin my song, and wish it may be so well liked.

THE ANGLER'S SONG.

As inward love breeds outward talk,
The hound some praise, and some the hawk,
Some, better pleas'd with private sport,
Use tennis, some a mistress court:
    But these delights I neither wish,
    Nor envy, while I freely fish.

Who hunts, doth oft in danger ride;
Who hawks, lures oft both far and wide
Who uses games shall often prove
A loser; but who falls in love,
    Is fetter'd in fond Cupid's snare:
    My angle breeds me no such care.

Of recreation there is none
So free as fishing is alone;
All other pastimes do no less
Than mind and body both possess:
    My hand alone my work can do,
    So I can fish and study too.

I care not, I, to fish in seas,
Fresh rivers best my mind do please,
Whose sweet calm course I contemplate,
And seek in life to imitate:
    In civil bounds I fain would keep,
    And for my past offences weep.

And when the timorous Trout I wait
To take, and he devours my bait,
How poor a thing, sometimes I find,
Will captivate a greedy mind:
    And when none bite, I praise the wise
    Whom vain allurements ne'er surprise.

But yet, though while I fish, I fast,
I make good fortune my repast;
And thereunto my friend invite,
In whom I more than that delight:
    Who is more welcome to my dish
    Than to my angle was my fish.

As well content no prize to take,
As use of taken prize to make:
For so our Lord was pleased, when
He fishers made fishers of men;
    Where, which is in no other game,
    A man may fish and praise his name.

The first men that our Saviour dear
Did choose to wait upon him here,
Blest fishers were, and fish the last
Food was that he on earth did taste:
    I therefore strive to follow those
    Whom he to follow him hath chose.

W. B.

CORIDON. Well sung, brother, you have paid your debt in good coin. We anglers are all beholden to the good man that made this song: come, hostess, give us more ale, and let's drink to him. And now let's every one go to bed, that we may rise early: but first let's pay our reckoning, for I will have nothing to hinder me in the morning; for my purpose is to prevent the sun-rising.

PETER. A match. Come, Coridon, you are to be my bed-fellow. I know, brother, you and your scholar will lie together. But where shall we meet to-morrow night? for my friend Coridon and I will go up the water towards Ware.

PISCATOR. And my scholar and I will go down towards Waltham.

CORIDON. Then let's meet here, for here are fresh sheets that smell of lavender; and I am sure we cannot expect better meat, or better usage in any place.

PETER. 'Tis a match. Good-night to everybody.

PISCATOR. And so say I.

VENATOR. And so say I.

## THE FOURTH DAY

PISCATOR. Good-morrow, good hostess, I see my brother Peter is still in bed. Come, give my scholar and me a morning drink, and a bit of meat to breakfast: and be sure to get a dish of meat or two against supper, for we shall come home as hungry as hawks. Come, scholar, let's be going.

VENATOR. Well now, good master, as we walk towards the river, give me direction, according to your promise, how I shall fish for a Trout.

PISCATOR. My honest scholar, I will take this very convenient opportunity to do it.

The Trout is usually caught with a worm, or a minnow, which some call a penk, or with a fly, *viz.* either a natural or an artificial fly: concerning which three, I will give you some observations and directions.

And, first, for worms. Of these there be very many sorts: some breed only in the earth, as the earth-worm; others of, or amongst plants, as the dug-worm; and others breed either out of excrements, or in the bodies of living creatures, as in the horns of sheep or deer; or some of dead flesh, as the maggot or gentle, and others.

Now these be most of them particularly good for particular fishes. But for the Trout, the dew-worm, which some also call the lob-worm, and the brandling, are the chief; and especially the first for a great Trout, and the latter for a less. There be also of lob-worms, some called squirrel-tails, a worm that has a red head, a streak down the back, and a broad tail, which are noted to be the best, because they are the toughest and most lively, and live longest in the water; for you are to know that a dead worm is but a dead bait, and like to catch nothing, compared to a lively, quick, stirring worm. And for a brandling, he is usually found in an old dunghill, or some very rotten place near to it, but most usually in cow-dung, or hog's-dung, rather than horse-dung, which is somewhat too hot and dry for that worm. But the best of them are to be found in the bark of the tanners, which they cast up in heaps after they have used it about their leather.

There are also divers other kinds of worms, which, for colour and shape, alter even as the ground out of which they are got; as the marsh-worm, the tag-tail, the flag-worm, the dock-worm, the oak-worm, the gilt-tail, the twachel or lob-worm, which of all others is the most excellent bait for a salmon, and too many to name, even as many sorts as some think there be of several herbs or shrubs, or of several kinds of birds in the air: of which I shall say no more, but tell you, that what worms soever you fish with, are the better for being well scoured, that is, long kept before they be used: and in case you have not been so provident, then the way to cleanse and scour them quickly, is, to put them all night in water, if they be lob-worms, and then put them into your bag with fennel. But you must not put your brandlings above an hour in water, and then put them into fennel, for sudden use: but if you have time, and purpose to keep them long, then they be best preserved in an earthen pot, with good store of moss, which is to be fresh every three or four days in summer, and every week or eight days in winter; or, at least, the moss taken from them, and clean washed, and wrung betwixt your hands till it be dry, and then put it to them again. And when your worms, especially the brandling, begins to be sick and lose of his bigness, then you may recover him, by putting a little milk or cream, about a spoonful in a day, into them, by drops on the moss; and if there be added to the cream an egg beaten and boiled in it, then it will both fatten and preserve them long. And note, that when the knot, which is near to the middle of the brandling, begins to swell, then he is sick; and, if he be not well looked to, is near dying. And for moss, you are to note, that there be divers kinds of it, which I could name to you, but I will only tell you that that which is likest a buck's-horn is the best, except it be soft white moss, which grows on some heaths, and is hard to be found. And note, that in a very dry time, when you are put to an extremity for worms, walnut-tree leaves squeezed into water, or salt in water, to make it bitter or salt, and then that water poured on the ground where you shall see worms are used to rise in the night, will make them to appear above ground presently. And you may take notice, some say that camphire put into your bag with your moss and worms gives them a strong and so tempting a smell, that the fish fare the worse and you the better for it.

And now, I shall shew you how to bait your hook with a worm so as shall prevent you from much trouble, and the loss of many a hook, too, when you fish for a Trout with a running line; that is to say, when you fish for him by hand at the ground. I will direct you in this as plainly as I can, that you may not mistake.

Suppose it be a big lob-worm: put your hook into him somewhat above the middle, and out again a little below the middle: having so done, draw your worm above the arming of your hook; but note, that, at the entering of your hook, it must not be at the head-end of the worm, but at the tail-end of him, that the point of your hook may come out toward the head-end; and, having drawn him above the arming of your hook, then put the point of your hook again into the very head of the worm, till it come near to the place where the point of the hook first came out, and then draw back that part of the worm that was above the shank or arming of your hook, and so fish with it. And if you mean to fish with two worms, then put the second on before you turn back the hook's-head of the first worm. You cannot lose above two or three worms before you attain to what I direct you; and having attained it, you will find it very useful, and thank me for it: for you will run on the ground without tangling.

Now for the Minnow or Penk: he is not easily found and caught till March, or in April, for then he appears first in the river; nature having taught him to shelter and hide himself, in the winter, in ditches that be near to the river; and there both to hide, and keep himself warm, in the mud, or in the weeds, which rot not so soon as in a running river, in which place if he were in winter, the distempered floods that are usually in that season would suffer him to take no rest, but carry him headlong to mills and weirs, to his confusion. And of these Minnows: first, you are to know, that the biggest size is not the best; and next, that the middle size and the whitest are the best; and then you are to know, that your minnow must be so put on your hook, that it must turn round when 'tis drawn against the stream; and, that it may turn nimbly, you must put it on a big-sized hook, as I shall now direct you, which is thus: Put your hook in at his mouth, and out at his gill; then, having drawn your hook two or three inches beyond or through his gill, put it again into his mouth, and the point and beard out at his tail; and then tie the hook and his tail about, very neatly, with a white thread, which will make it the apter to turn quick in the water; that done, pull back that part of your line which was slack when you did put your hook into the minnow the second time; I say, pull that part of your line back, so that it shall fasten the head, so that the body of the minnow shall be almost straight on your hook: this done, try how it will turn, by drawing it across the water or against a stream; and if it do not turn nimbly, then turn the tail a little to the right or left hand, and try again, till it turn quick; for if not, you are in danger to catch nothing: for know, that it is impossible that it should turn too quick. And you are yet to know, that in case you want a minnow, then a small loach, or a stickle-bag, or any other small fish that will turn quick, will serve as well. And you are yet to know that you may salt them, and by that means keep them ready and fit for use three or four days, or longer; and that, of salt, bay-salt is the best.

And here let me tell you, what many old anglers know right well, that at some times, and in some waters, a minnow is not to be got; and therefore, let me tell you, I have, which I will shew to you, an artificial minnow, that will catch a Trout as well as an artificial fly: and it was made by a handsome woman that had a fine hand, and a live minnow lying by her: the mould or body of the minnow was cloth, and wrought upon, or over it, thus, with a needle; the back of it with very sad French green silk, and paler green silk towards the belly, shadowed as perfectly as you can imagine, just as you see a minnow: the belly was wrought also with a needle, and it was, a part of it, white silk; and another part of it with silver thread: the tail and fins were of a quill, which was shaven thin: the eyes were of two little black beads: and the head was so shadowed, and all of it so curiously wrought, and so exactly dissembled, that it would beguile any sharp-sighted Trout in a swift stream. And this minnow I will now shew you; look, here it is, and, if you like it, lend it you, to have two or three made by it; for they be easily carried about an angler, and be of excellent use: for note, that a large Trout will come as fiercely at a minnow as the highest-mettled hawk doth seize on a partridge, or a greyhound on a hare. I have been told that one hundred and sixty minnows have been found in a Trout's belly: either the Trout had devoured so many, or the miller that gave it a friend of mine had forced them down his throat after he had taken him.

Now for Flies; which is the third bait wherewith Trouts are usually taken. You are to know, that there are so many sorts of flies as there be of fruits: I will name you but some of them; as the dun-fly, the stone-fly, the red-fly, the moor-fly, the tawny-fly, the shell-fly, the cloudy or blackish-fly, the flag-fly, the vine-fly; there be of flies, caterpillars, and canker-flies, and bear-flies; and indeed too many either for me to name, or for you to remember. And their breeding is so various and wonderful, that I might easily amaze myself, and tire you in a relation of them.

And, yet, I will exercise your promised patience by saying a little of the caterpillar, or the palmer-fly or worm; that by them you may guess what a work it were, in a discourse, but to run over those very many flies, worms, and little living creatures, with which the sun and summer adorn and beautify the river-banks and meadows, both for the recreation and contemplation of us anglers; pleasures which, I think, myself enjoy more than any other man that is not of my profession.

Pliny holds an opinion, that many have their birth, or being, from a dew that in the spring falls upon the leaves of trees; and that some kinds of them are from a dew left upon herbs or flowers; and others from a dew left upon coleworts or cabbages: all which kinds of dews being thickened and condensed, are by the sun's generative heat, most of them, hatched, and in three days made living creatures: and these of several shapes and colours; some being hard and tough, some smooth and soft; some are horned in their head, some in their tail, some have none; some have hair, some none: some have sixteen feet, some less, and some have none: but, as our Topsel hath with great diligence observed, those which have none, move upon the earth, or upon broad leaves, their motion being not unlike to the waves of the sea. Some of them he also observes to be bred of the eggs of other caterpillars, and that those in their time turn to be butterflies; and again, that their eggs turn the following year to be caterpillars. And some affirm, that every plant has its particular fly or caterpillar, which it breeds and feeds. I have seen, and may therefore affirm it, a green caterpillar, or worm, as big as a small peascod, which had fourteen legs; eight on the belly, four under the neck, and two near the tail. It was found on a hedge of privet; and was taken thence, and put into a large box, and a little branch or two of privet put to it, on which I saw it feed as sharply as a dog gnaws a bone: it lived thus, five or six days, and thrived, and changed the colour two or three times, but by some neglect in the keeper of it, it then died, and did not turn to a fly: but if it had lived, it had doubtless turned to one of those flies that some call Flies of prey, which those that walk by the rivers may, in summer, see fasten on smaller flies, and, I think, make them their food. And 'tis observable, that as there be these flies of prey, which be very large; so there be others, very little, created, I think, only to feed them, and breed out of I know not what; whose life, they say, nature intended not to exceed an hour; and yet that life is thus made shorter by other flies, or accident.

'Tis endless to tell you what the curious searchers into nature's productions have observed of these worms and flies: but yet I shall tell you what Aldrovandus, our Topsel, and others, say of the Palmer-worm, or Caterpillar: that whereas others content themselves to feed on particular herbs or leaves; for most think, those very leaves that gave them life and shape, give them a particular feeding and nourishment, and that upon them they usually abide; yet he observes, that this is called a pilgrim, or palmer-worm, for his very wandering life, and various food; not contenting himself, as others do, with any one certain place for his abode, nor any certain kind of herb or flower for his feeding, but will boldly and disorderly wander up and down, and not endure to be kept to a diet, or fixt to a particular place.

Nay, the very colours of caterpillars are, as one has observed, very elegant and beautiful. I shall, for a taste of the rest, describe one of them; which I will, some time the next month, shew you feeding on a willow-tree; and you shall find him punctually to answer this very description: his lips and mouth somewhat yellow; his eyes black as jet; his forehead purple; his feet and hinder parts green; his tail two-forked and black; the whole body stained with a kind of red spots, which run along the neck and shoulder-blade, not unlike the form of St. Andrew's cross, or the letter X, made thus crosswise, and a white line drawn down his back to his tail; all which add much beauty to his whole body. And it is to me observable, that at a fixed age this caterpillar gives over to eat, and towards winter comes to be covered over with a strange shell or crust, called an aurelia; and so lives a kind of dead life, without eating all the winter. And as others of several kinds turn to be several kinds of flies and vermin, the Spring following; so this caterpillar then turns to be a painted butterfly.

Come, come, my scholar, you see the river stops our morning walk: and I will also here stop my discourse: only as we sit down under this honeysuckle hedge, whilst I look a line to fit the rod that our brother Peter hath lent you, I shall, for a little confirmation of what I have said, repeat the observation of Du Bartas:

> God, not contented to each kind to give
> And to infuse the virtue generative,
> Made, by his wisdom, many creatures breed
> Of lifeless bodies, without Venus' deed.
>
> So, the cold humour breeds the Salamander,
> Who, in effect, like to her birth's commander,
> With child with hundred winters, with her touch
> Quencheth the fire, tho' glowing ne'er so much.
>
> So of the fire, in burning furnace, springs
> The fly Pyrausta with the flaming wings:
> Without the fire, it dies: within it joys,
> Living in that which each thing else destroys.
>
> So, slow Boôtes underneath him sees,
> In th' icy isles, those goslings hatch'd of trees;
> Whose fruitful leaves, falling into the water,
> Are turn'd, they say, to living fowls soon after.
>
> So, rotten sides of broken ships do change
> To barnacles. O transformation strange!
> 'Twas first a green tree; then, a gallant hull;
> Lately a mushroom; now, a flying gull.

VENATOR. O my good master, this morning-walk has been spent to my great pleasure and wonder: but, I pray, when shall I have your direction how to make artificial flies, like to those that the Trout loves best; and, also, how to use them?

PISCATOR. My honest scholar, it is now past five of the clock: we will fish till nine; and then go to breakfast. Go you to yonder sycamore-tree, and hide your bottle of drink under the hollow root of it; for about that time, and in that place, we will make a brave breakfast with a piece of powdered beef, and a radish or two, that I have in my fish bag: we shall, I warrant you, make a good, honest, wholesome hungry breakfast. And I will then give you direction for the making and using of your flies: and in the meantime, there is your rod and line; and my advice is, that you fish as you see me do, and let's try which can catch the first fish.

VENATOR. I thank you, master. I will observe and practice your direction as far as I am able.

PISCATOR. Look you, scholar; you see I have hold of a good fish: I now see it is a Trout. I pray, put that net under him; and touch not my line, for if you do, then we break all. Well done, scholar: I thank you.

Now for another. Trust me, I have another bite. Come, scholar, come lay down your rod, and help me to land this as you did the other. So now we shall be sure to have a good dish of fish for supper.

VENATOR. I am glad of that: but I have no fortune: sure, master, yours is a better rod and better tackling.

PISCATOR. Nay, then, take mine; and I will fish with yours. Look you, scholar, I have another. Come, do as you did before. And now I have a bite at another. Oh me! he has broke all: there's half a line and a good hook lost.

VENATOR. Ay, and a good Trout too.

PISCATOR. Nay, the Trout is not lost; for pray take notice, no man can lose what he never had.

VENATOR. Master, I can neither catch with the first nor second angle: I have no fortune.

PISCATOR. Look you, scholar, I have yet another. And now, having caught three brace of Trouts, I will tell you a short tale as we walk towards our breakfast. A scholar, a preacher I should say, that was to preach to procure the approbation of a parish that he might be their lecturer, had got from his fellow-pupil the copy of a sermon that was first preached with great commendation by him that composed it: and though the borrower of it preached it, word for word, as it was at first, yet it was utterly disliked as it was preached by the second to his congregation, which the sermon-borrower complained of to the lender of it: and was thus answered: "I lent you, indeed, my fiddle, but not my fiddle-stick; for you are to know, that every one cannot make musick with my words, which are fitted for my own mouth." And so, my scholar, you are to know, that as the ill pronunciation or ill accenting of words in a sermon spoils it, so the ill carriage of your line, or not fishing even to a foot in a right place, makes you lose your labour: and you are to know, that though you have my fiddle, that is, my very rod and tacklings with which you see I catch fish, yet you have not my fiddle-stick, that is, you yet have not skill to know how to carry your hand and line, nor how to guide it to a right place: and this must be taught you;

for you are to remember, I told you Angling is an art, either by practice or a long observation, or both. But take this for a rule, When you fish for a Trout with a worm, let your line have so much, and not more lead than will fit the stream in which you fish; that is to say, more in a great troublesome stream than in a smaller that is quieter; as near as may be, so much as will sink the bait to the bottom, and keep it still in motion, and not more.

But now, let's say grace, and fall to breakfast. What say you, scholar, to the providence of an old angler? Does not this meat taste well? and was not this place well chosen to eat it? for this sycamore-tree will shade us from the sun's heat.

VENATOR. All excellent good; and my stomach excellent good, too. And now I remember, and find that true which devout Lessius says, "that poor men, and those that fast often, have much more pleasure in eating than rich men, and gluttons, that always feed before their stomachs are empty of their last meat and call for more; for by that means they rob themselves of that pleasure that hunger brings to poor men." And I do seriously approve of that saying of yours, "that you had rather be a civil, well-governed, well-grounded, temperate, poor angler, than a drunken lord": but I hope there is none such. However, I am certain of this, that I have been at many very costly dinners that have not afforded me half the content that this has done; for which I thank God and you.

And now, good master, proceed to your promised direction for making and ordering my artificial fly.

PISCATOR. My honest scholar, I will do it; for it is a debt due unto you by my promise. And because you shall not think yourself more engaged to me than indeed you really are, I will freely give you such directions as were lately given to me by an ingenious brother of the angle, an honest man, and a most excellent fly-fisher.

You are to note, that there are twelve kinds of artificial made Flies, to angle with upon the top of the water. Note, by the way, that the fittest season of using these is in a blustering windy day, when the waters are so troubled that the natural fly cannot be seen, or rest upon them. The first is the dun-fly, in March: the body is made of dun wool; the wings, of the partridge's feathers. The second is another dun-fly: the body, of black wool; and the wings made of the black drake's feathers, and of the feathers under his tail. The third is the stone-fly, in April: the body is made of black wool; made yellow under the wings and under the tail, and so made with wings of the drake. The fourth is the ruddy-fly, in the beginning of May: the body made of red wool, wrapt about with black silk; and the feathers are the wings of the drake; with the feathers of a red capon also, which hang dangling on his sides next to the tail. The fifth is the yellow or greenish fly, in May likewise: the body made of yellow wool; and the wings made of the red cock's hackle or tail. The sixth is the black-fly, in May also: the body made of black wool, and lapt about with the herle of a peacock's tail: the wings are made of the wings of a brown capon, with his blue feathers in his head. The seventh is the sad yellow-fly in June: the body is made of black wool, with a yellow list on either side; and the wings taken off the wings of a buzzard, bound with black braked hemp. The eighth is the moorish-fly; made, with the body, of duskish wool; and the wings made of the blackish mail of the drake. The ninth is the tawny-fly, good until the middle of June: the body made of tawny wool; the wings made contrary one against the other, made of the whitish mail of the wild drake. The tenth is the wasp-fly in July; the body made of black wool, lapt about with yellow silk; the wings made of the feathers of the drake, or of the buzzard. The eleventh is the shell-fly, good in mid-July: the body made of greenish wool, lapt about with the herle of a peacock's tail: and the wings made of the wings of the buzzard. The twelfth is the dark drake-fly, good in August: the body made with black wool, lapt about with black silk; his wings are made with the mail of the black drake, with a black head. Thus have you a jury of flies, likely to betray and condemn all the Trouts in the river.

I shall next give you some other directions for fly-fishing, such as are given by Mr. Thomas Barker, a gentleman that hath spent much time in fishing: but I shall do it with a little variation.

First, let your rod be light, and very gentle: I take the best to be of two pieces. And let not your line exceed, especially for three or four links next to the hook, I say, not exceed three or four hairs at the most; though you may fish a little stronger above, in the upper part of your line: but if you can attain to angle with one hair, you shall have more rises, and catch more fish. Now you must be sure not to cumber yourself with too long a line, as most do. And before you begin to angle, cast to have the wind on your back; and the sun, if it shines, to be before you; and to fish down the stream; and carry the point or top of your rod downward, by which means the shadow of yourself, and rod too, will be the least offensive to the fish; for the sight of any shade amazes the fish, and spoils your sport, of which you must take great care.

In the middle of March, till which time a man should not in honesty catch a Trout; or in April, if the weather be dark, or a little windy or cloudy; the best fishing is with the palmer-worm, of which I last spoke to you; but of these there be divers kinds, or at least of divers colours: these and the May-fly are the ground of all fly-angling: which are to be thus made:

First, you must arm your hook with the line, in the inside of it: then take your scissors, and cut so much of a brown mallard's feather as, in your own reason, will make the wings of it, you having, withal, regard to the bigness or littleness of your hook; then lay the outmost part of your feather next to your hook; then the point of your feather next the shank of your hook, and, having so done, whip it three or four times about the hook with the same silk with which your hook was armed; and having made the silk fast, take the hackle of a cock or capon's neck, or a plover's top, which is usually better: take off the one side of the feather, and then take the hackle, silk or crewel, gold or silver thread; make these fast at the bent of the hook, that is to say, below your arming; then you must take the hackle, the silver or gold thread, and work it up to the wings, shifting or still removing your finger as you turn the silk about the hook, and still looking, at every stop or turn, that your gold, or what materials soever you make your fly of, do lie right and neatly; and if you find they do so, then when you have made the head, make all fast: and then work your hackle up to the head, and make that fast: and then, with a needle, or pin, divide the wing into two; and then, with the arming silk, whip it about cross-ways betwixt the wings: and then with your thumb you must turn the point of the feather towards the bent of the hook; and then work three or four times about the shank of the hook; and then view the proportion; and if all be neat, and to your liking, fasten.

I confess, no direction can be given to make a man of a dull capacity able to make a fly well: and yet I know this, with a little practice, will help an ingenious angler in a good degree. But to see a fly made by an artist in that kind, is the best teaching to make it. And, then, an ingenious angler may walk by the river, and mark what flies fall on the water that day; and catch one of them, if he sees the Trouts leap at a fly of that kind: and then having always hooks ready-hung with him, and having a bag always with him, with bear's hair, or the hair of a brown or sad-coloured heifer, hackles of a cock or capon, several coloured silk and crewel to make the body of the fly, the feathers of a drake's head, black or brown sheep's wool, or hog's wool, or hair, thread of gold and of silver; silk of several colours, especially sad-coloured, to make the fly's head: and there be also other coloured feathers, both of little birds and of speckled fowl: I say, having those with him in a bag, and trying to make a fly, though he miss at first, yet shall he at last hit it better, even to such a perfection as none can well teach him. And if he hit to make his fly right, and have the luck to hit, also, where there is store of Trouts, a dark day, and a right wind, he will catch such store of them, as will encourage him to grow more and more in love with the art of fly-making.

VENATOR. But, my loving master, if any wind will not serve, then I wish I were in Lapland, to buy a good wind of one of the honest witches, that sell so many winds there, and so cheap.

PISCATOR. Marry, scholar, but I would not be there, nor indeed from under this tree; for look how it begins to rain, and by the clouds, if I mistake not, we shall presently have a smoking shower, and therefore sit close; this sycamore-tree will shelter us: and I will tell you, as they shall come into my mind, more observations of fly-fishing for a Trout.

But first for the wind: you are to take notice that of the winds the south wind is said to be best. One observes, that

when the wind is south,
It blows your bait into a fish's mouth.

Next to that, the west wind is believed to be the best: and having told you that the east wind is the worst, I need not tell you which wind is the best in the third degree: and yet, as Solomon observes, that "he that considers the wind shall never sow"; so he that busies his head too much about them, if the weather be not made extreme cold by an east wind, shall be a little superstitious: for as it is observed by some, that "there is no good horse of a bad colour"; so I have observed, that if it be a cloudy day, and not extreme cold, let the wind sit in what corner it will and do its worst, I heed it not. And yet take this for a rule, that I would willingly fish, standing on the lee-shore: and you are to take notice, that the fish lies or swims nearer the bottom, and in deeper water, in winter than in summer; and also nearer the bottom in any cold day, and then gets nearest the lee-side of the water.

But I promised to tell you more of the Fly-fishing for a Trout; which I may have time enough to do, for you see it rains May butter. First for a Mayfly: you may make his body with greenish-coloured crewel, or willowish colour; darkening it in most places with waxed silk; or ribbed with black hair; or, some of them, ribbed with silver thread; and such wings, for the colour, as you see the fly to have at that season, nay, at that very day on the water. Or you may make the Oak-fly: with an orange, tawny, and black ground; and the brown of a mallard's feather for the wings. And you are to know, that these two are most excellent flies, that is, the May-fly and the Oak-fly.

And let me again tell you, that you keep as far from the water as you can possibly, whether you fish with a fly or worm; and fish down the stream. And when you fish with a fly, if it be possible, let no part of your line touch the water, but your fly only; and be still moving your fly upon the water, or casting it into the water, you yourself being also always moving down the stream.

Mr. Barker commends several sorts of the palmer-flies; not only those ribbed with silver and gold, but others that have their bodies all made of black; or some with red, and a red hackle. You may also make the Hawthorn-fly: which is all black, and not big, but very small, the smaller the better. Or the oak-fly, the body of which is orange colour and black crewel, with a brown wing. Or a fly made with a peacock's feather is excellent in a bright day: you must be sure you want not in your magazine-bag the peacock's feather; and grounds of such wool and crewel as will make the grasshopper. And note, that usually the smallest flies are the best; and note also, that the light fly does usually make most sport in a dark day, and the darkest and least fly in a bright or clear day: and lastly note, that you are to repair upon any occasion to your magazine-bag: and upon any occasion, vary and make them lighter or sadder, according to your fancy, or the day.

And now I shall tell you, that the fishing with a natural-fly is excellent, and affords much pleasure. They may be found thus: the May-fly, usually in and about that month, near to the river-side, especially against rain: the Oak-fly, on the butt or body of an oak or ash, from the beginning of May to the end of August; it is a brownish fly and easy to be so found, and stands usually with his head downward, that is to say, towards the root of the tree: the small black-fly, or Hawthorn-fly, is to be had on any hawthorn bush after the leaves be come forth. With these and a short line, as I shewed to angle for a Chub, you may dape or dop, and also with a grasshopper, behind a tree, or in any deep hole; still making it to move on the top of the water as if it were alive, and still keeping yourself out of sight, you shall certainly have sport if there be Trouts; yea, in a hot day, but especially in the evening of a hot day, you will have sport.

And now, scholar, my direction for fly-fishing is ended with this shower, for it has done raining. And now look about you, and see how pleasantly that meadow looks; nay, and the earth smells so sweetly too. Come let me tell you what holy Mr. Herbert says of such days and flowers as these, and then we will thank God that we enjoy them, and walk to the river and sit down quietly, and try to catch the other brace of Trouts.

Sweet day, so cool, so calm, so bright,
The bridal of the earth and sky,
Sweet dews shall weep thy fall to-night,
For thou must die.

Sweet rose, whose hue, angry and brave,
Bids the rash gazer wipe his eye,
Thy root is ever in its grave,
And thou must die.

Sweet spring, full of sweet days and roses,

A box where sweets compacted lie;
My music shews you have your closes,
And all must die.

Only a sweet and virtuous soul,
Like season'd timber, never gives,
But when the whole world turns to coal,
Then chiefly lives.

VENATOR. I thank you, good master, for your good direction for fly-fishing, and for the sweet enjoyment of the pleasant day, which is so far spent without offence to God or man: and I thank you for the sweet close of your discourse with Mr. Herbert's verses; who, I have heard, loved angling; and I do the rather believe it, because he had a spirit suitable to anglers, and to those primitive Christians that you love, and have so much commended.

PISCATOR. Well, my loving scholar, and I am pleased to know that you are so well pleased with my direction and discourse.

And since you like these verses of Mr. Herbert's so well, let me tell you what a reverend and learned divine that professes to imitate him, and has indeed done so most excellently, hath writ of our book of Common Prayer; which I know you will like the better, because he is a friend of mine, and I am sure no enemy to angling.

What! Pray'r by th' book? and Common? Yes; Why not?
The spirit of grace
And supplication
Is not left free alone
For time and place,
But manner too: to read, or speak, by rote,
Is all alike to him that prays,
In's heart, what with his mouth he says.

They that in private, by themselves alone,
Do pray, may take
What liberty they please,
In chusing of the ways
Wherein to make
Their soul's most intimate affections known
To him that sees in secret, when
Th' are most conceal'd from other men.

But he, that unto others leads the way
In public prayer,
Should do it so,
As all, that hear, may know
They need not fear
To tune their hearts unto his tongue, and say

Amen; not doubt they were betray'd
To blaspheme, when they meant to have pray'd.

Devotion will add life unto the letter:
And why should not
That, which authority
Prescribes, esteemed be
Advantage got?
If th' prayer be good, the commoner the better,
Prayer in the Church's words, as well
As sense, of all prayers bears the bell.

CH. HARVIE.

And now, scholar, I think it will be time to repair to our angle-rods, which we left in the water to fish for themselves; and you shall choose which shall be yours; and it is an even lay, one of them catches.

And, let me tell you, this kind of fishing with a dead rod, and laying night-hooks, are like putting money to use; for they both work for the owners when they do nothing but sleep, or eat, or rejoice, as you know we have done this last hour, and sat as quietly and as free from cares under this sycamore, as Virgil's Tityrus and his Melibœus did under their broad beech-tree. No life, my honest scholar, no life so happy and so pleasant as the life of a well-governed angler; for when the lawyer is swallowed up with business, and the statesman is preventing or contriving plots, then we sit on cowslip-banks, hear the birds sing, and possess ourselves in as much quietness as these silent silver streams, which we now see glide so quietly by us. Indeed, my good scholar, we may say of angling, as Dr. Boteler said of strawberries, "Doubtless God could have made a better berry, but doubtless God never did"; and so, if I might be judge, God never did make a more calm, quiet, innocent recreation than angling.

I'll tell you, scholar; when I sat last on this primrose-bank, and looked down these meadows, I thought of them as Charles the emperor did of the city of Florence: "That they were too pleasant to be looked on, but only on holy-days." As I then sat on this very grass, I turned my present thoughts into verse: 'twas a Wish, which I'll repeat to you:—

### THE ANGLER'S WISH.

I in these flowery meads would be:
These crystal streams should solace me;
To whose harmonious bubbling noise
I with my Angle would rejoice:
Sit here, and see the turtle-dove
Court his chaste mate to acts of love:

Or, on that bank, feel the west wind
Breathe health and plenty: please my mind,
To see sweet dew-drops kiss these flowers,
And then washed off by April showers:
Here, hear my Kenna sing[1] a song;
There, see a blackbird feed her young,

Or a leverock build her nest:
Here, give my weary spirits rest,
And raise my low-pitch'd thoughts above
Earth, or what poor mortals love:
  Thus, free from law-suits and the noise
  Of princes' courts, I would rejoice:

Or, with my Bryan, and a book,
Loiter long days near Shawford-brook;
There sit by him, and eat my meat,
There see the sun both rise and set:
There bid good morning to next day;
There meditate my time away,
  And Angle on; and beg to have
  A quiet passage to a welcome grave.

When I had ended this composure, I left this place, and saw a brother of the angle sit under that honeysuckle hedge, one that will prove worth your acquaintance. I sat down by him, and presently we met with an accidental piece of merriment, which I will relate to you, for it rains still.

On the other side of this very hedge sat a gang of gypsies; and near to them sat a gang of beggars. The gypsies were then to divide all the money that had been got that week, either by stealing linen or poultry, or by fortune-telling or legerdemain, or, indeed, by any other sleights and secrets belonging to their mysterious government. And the sum that was got that week proved to be but twenty and some odd shillings. The odd money was agreed to be distributed amongst the poor of their own corporation: and for the remaining twenty shillings, that was to be divided unto four gentlemen gypsies, according to their several degrees in their commonwealth. And the first or chiefest gypsy was, by consent, to have a third part of the twenty shillings, which all men know is 6*s.* 8*d.* The second was to have a fourth part of the 20*s.*, which all men know to be 5*s.* The third was to have a fifth part of the 20*s.*, which all men know to be 4*s.* The fourth and last gypsy was to have a sixth part of the 20*s.*, which all men know to be 3*s.* 4*d.*

[1]Like Hermit Poor.

As for example,

| | |
|---|---|
| 3 times 6s. 8*d*. are. . . . . . . . . . . | 20s. |
| And so is 4 times 5s. . . . . . . . . . | 20s. |
| And so is 5 times 4s. . . . . . . . . . | 20s. |
| And so is 6 times 3s. 4*d*. . . . . . . . | 20s. |

And yet he that divided the money was so very a gypsy, that though he gave to every one these said sums, yet he kept one shilling of it for himself.

| | s. | *d.* |
|---|---|---|
| As, for example, | | |
| | 6 | 8 |
| | 5 | 0 |
| | 4 | 0 |
| | 3 | 4 |
| make but . . . . . . . . . . . . . . | 19 | 0 |

But now you shall know, that when the four gypsies saw that he had got one shilling by dividing the money, though not one of them knew any reason to demand more, yet, like lords and courtiers, every gypsy envied him that was the gainer; and wrangled with him; and every one said the remaining shilling belonged to him; and so they fell to so high a contest about it, as none that knows the faithfulness of one gypsy to another will easily believe; only we that have lived these last twenty years are certain that money has been able to do much mischief. However, the gypsies were too wise to go to law, and did therefore choose their choice friends Rook and Shark, and our late English Gusman, to be their arbitrators and umpires. And so they left this honeysuckle hedge; and went to tell fortunes and cheat, and get more money and lodging in the next village.

When these were gone, we heard as high a contention amongst the beggars, whether it was easiest to rip a cloak, or to unrip a cloak? One beggar affirmed it was all one: but that was denied, by asking her, If doing and undoing were all one? Then another said, 'twas easiest to unrip a cloak; for that was to let it alone: but she was answered, by asking her, how she unript it if she let it alone? and she confest herself mistaken. These and twenty such like questions were proposed and answered, with as much beggarly logick and earnestness as was ever heard to proceed from the mouth of the pertinacious schismatick; and sometimes all the beggars, whose number was neither more nor less than the poets' nine muses, talked all together about this ripping and unripping; and so loud, that not one heard what the other said: but, at last, one beggar craved audience; and told them that old father Clause, whom Ben Jonson, in his Beggar's Bush, created King of their corporation, was to lodge at an ale-house, called "Catch-her-by-the-way," not far from Waltham Cross, and in the high road towards London; and he therefore desired them to spend no more time about that and such like questions, but refer all to father Clause at night, for he was an upright judge, and in the meantime draw cuts, what song should be next sung, and who should sing it. They all agreed to the motion; and the lot fell to her that was the youngest, and veriest virgin of the company. And she sung Frank Davison's song, which he made forty years ago; and all the others of the company joined to sing the burthen with her. The ditty was this; but first the burthen:

Bright shines the sun; play, Beggars, play;
Here's scraps enough to serve to-day.

What noise of viols is so sweet,
As when our merry clappers ring?
What mirth doth want where Beggars meet?
A Beggar's life is for a King.
Eat, drink, and play; sleep when we list;
Go where we will, so stocks be mist.
Bright shines the sun; play, Beggars, play;
Here's scraps enough to serve to-day.

The world is ours, and ours alone;
For we alone have world at will;
We purchase not; all is our own;
Both fields and streets we Beggars fill.
Nor care to get, nor fear to keep,
Did ever break a Beggar's sleep.
Play, Beggars, play; play, Beggars, play;
Here's scraps enough to serve to-day.

A hundred head of black and white
Upon our gowns securely feed;
If any dare his master bite,
He dies therefore, as sure as creed.
Thus Beggars lord it as they please;
And only Beggars live at ease.
Bright shines the sun; play, Beggars, play;
Here's scraps enough to serve to-day.

VENATOR. I thank you, good master, for this piece of merriment, and this song, which was well humoured by the maker, and well remembered by you.

PISCATOR. But, I pray, forget not the catch which you promised to make against night; for our countryman, honest Coridon, will expect your catch, and my song, which I must be forced to patch up, for it is so long since I learnt it, that I have forgot a part of it. But, come, now it hath done raining, let's stretch our legs a little in a gentle walk to the river, and try what interest our angles will pay us for lending them so long to be used by the Trouts; lent them indeed, like usurers, for our profit and their destruction.

VENATOR. Oh me! look you, master, a fish! a fish! Oh, alas, master, I have lost her.

PISCATOR. Ay marry, Sir, that was a good fish indeed: if I had had the luck to have taken up that rod, then 'tis twenty to one he should not have broken my line by running to the rod's end, as you suffered him. I would have held him within the bent of my rod, unless he had been fellow to the great Trout that is near an ell long, which was of such a length and depth, that he had his picture drawn, and now is to be seen at mine host Rickabie's, at the George in Ware, and it may be, by giving that very great Trout the rod, that is, by casting it to him into the water, I might have caught him at the long run, for so I use always to do when I meet with an over-grown fish; and you will learn to do so too, hereafter, for I tell you, scholar, fishing is an art, or, at least, it is an art to catch fish.

VENATOR. But, master, I have heard that the great Trout you speak of is a Salmon.

PISCATOR. Trust me, scholar, I know not what to say to it. There are many country people that believe hares change sexes every year: and there be very many learned men think so too, for in their dissecting them they find many reasons to incline them to that belief. And to make the wonder seem yet less, that hares change sexes, note that Dr. Mer. Casaubon affirms, in his book "Of credible and incredible things," that Gasper Peucerus, a learned physician, tells us of a people that once a year turn wolves, partly in shape, and partly in conditions. And so, whether this were a Salmon when he came into fresh water, and his not returning into the sea hath altered him to another colour or kind, I am not able to say; but I am certain he hath all the signs of being a Trout, both for his shape, colour, and spots; and yet many think he is not.

VENATOR. But, master, will this Trout which I had hold of die? for it is like he hath the hook in his belly.

PISCATOR. I will tell you, scholar, that unless the hook be fast in his very gorge, 'tis more than probable he will live, and a little time, with the help of the water, will rust the hook, and it will in time wear away, as the gravel doth in the horse-hoof, which only leaves a false quarter.

And now, scholar, let's go to my rod. Look you, scholar, I have a fish too, but it proves a logger-headed Chub: and this is not much amiss, for this will pleasure some poor body, as we go to our lodging to meet our brother Peter and honest Coridon. Come, now bait your hook again, and lay it into the water, for it rains again; and we will even retire to the Sycamore-tree, and there I will give you more directions concerning fishing, for I would fain make you an artist.

VENATOR. Yes, good master, I pray let it be so.

PISCATOR. Well, scholar, now that we are sate down and are at ease, I shall tell you a little more of Trout-fishing, before I speak of the Salmon, which I purpose shall be next, and then of the Pike or Luce.

You are to know, there is night as well as day fishing for a Trout; and that, in the night, the best Trouts come out of their holes. And the manner of taking them is on the top of the water with a great lob or garden-worm, or rather two, which you are to fish with in a stream where the waters run somewhat quietly, for in a stream the bait will not be so well discerned. I say, in a quiet or dead place, near to some swift, there draw your bait over the top of the water, to and fro, and if there be a good Trout in the hole, he will take it, especially if the night be dark, for then he is bold, and lies near the top of the water, watching the motion of any frog or water-rat, or mouse, that swims betwixt him and the sky; these he hunts after, if he sees the water but wrinkle or move in one of these dead holes, where these great old Trouts usually lie, near to their holds; for you are to note, that the great old Trout is both subtle and fearful, and lies close all day, and does not usually stir out of his hold, but lies in it as close in the day as the timorous hare does in her form; for the chief feeding of either is seldom in the day, but usually in the night, and then the great Trout feeds very boldly.

And you must fish for him with a strong line, and not a little hook; and let him have time to gorge your hook, for he does not usually forsake it, as he oft will in the day-fishing. And if the night be not dark, then fish so with an artificial fly of a light colour, and at the snap: nay, he will sometimes rise at a dead mouse, or a piece of cloth, or anything that seems to swim across the water, or to be in motion. This is a choice way, but I have not oft used it, because it is void of the pleasures that such days as these, that we two now enjoy, afford an angler.

And you are to know, that in Hampshire, which I think exceeds all England for swift, shallow, clear, pleasant brooks, and store of Trouts, they used to catch Trouts in the night, by the light of a torch or straw, which, when they have discovered, they strike with a Trout-spear, or other ways. This kind of way they catch very many: but I would not believe it till I was an eye-witness of it, nor do I like it now I have seen it.

VENATOR. But, master, do not Trouts see us in the night?

PISCATOR. Yes, and hear, and smell too, both then and in the day-time: for Gesner observes, the Otter smells a fish forty furlongs off him in the water: and that it may be true, seems to be affirmed by Sir Francis Bacon, in the eighth century of his *Natural History*, who there proves that waters may be the medium of sounds, by demonstrating it thus: "That if you knock two stones together very deep under the water, those that stand on a bank near to that place may hear the noise without any diminution of it by the water." He also offers the like experiment concerning the letting an anchor fall, by a very long cable or rope, on a rock, or the sand, within the sea. And this being so well observed and demonstrated as it is by that learned man, has made me to believe that Eels unbed themselves and stir at the noise of thunder, and not only, as some think, by the motion or stirring of the earth which is occasioned by that thunder.

And this reason of Sir Francis Bacon has made me crave pardon of one that I laughed at for affirming that he knew Carps come to a certain place, in a pond, to be fed at the ringing of a bell or the beating of a drum. And, however, it shall be a rule for me to make as little noise as I can when I am fishing, until Sir Francis Bacon be confuted, which I shall give any man leave to do.

And lest you may think him singular in this opinion, I will tell you, this seems to be believed by our learned Doctor Hakewill, who in his *Apology of God's power and providence*, quotes Pliny to report that one of the emperors had particular fish-ponds, and, in them, several fish that appeared and came when they were called by their particular names. And St. James tells us, that all things in the sea have been tamed by mankind. And Pliny tells us, that Antonia, the wife of Drusus, had a Lamprey at whose gills she hung jewels or ear-rings; and that others have been so tender-hearted as to shed tears at the death of fishes which they have kept and loved. And these observations, which will to most hearers seem wonderful, seem to have a further confirmation from Martial, who writes thus:—

*Piscator, fuge; ne nocens, etc.*

Angler! would'st thou be guiltless? then forbear;
For these are sacred fishes that swim here,
Who know their sovereign, and will lick his hand,
Than which none's greater in the world's command;
Nay more they've names, and, when they called are,
Do to their several owner's call repair.

All the further use that I shall make of this shall be, to advise anglers to be patient, and forbear swearing, lest they be heard, and catch no fish.

And so I shall proceed next to tell you, it is certain that certain fields near Leominster, a town in Herefordshire, are observed to make the sheep that graze upon them more fat than the next, and also to bear finer wool; that is to say, that that year in which they feed in such a particular pasture, they shall yield finer wool than they did that year before they came to feed in it; and coarser, again, if they shall return to their former pasture; and, again, return to a finer wool, being fed in the fine wool ground: which I tell you, that you may the better believe that I am certain, if I catch a Trout in one meadow, he shall be white and faint, and very like to be lousy; and, as certainly, if I catch a Trout in the next meadow, he shall be strong, and red, and lusty, and much better meat. Trust me, scholar, I have caught many a Trout in a particular meadow, that the very shape and the enamelled colour of him hath been such as hath joyed me to look on him: and I have then, with much pleasure, concluded with Solomon, "Everything is beautiful in his season."

I should, by promise, speak next of the Salmon; but I will, by your favour, say a little of the Umber or Grayling; which is so like a Trout for his shape and feeding, that I desire I may exercise your patience with a short discourse of him; and then, the next shall be of the Salmon.

# THE FOURTH DAY—*continued*

## *The Umber or Grayling*

### CHAPTER VI

PISCATOR

THE Umber and Grayling are thought by some to differ as the Herring and Pilchard do. But though they may do so in other nations, I think those in England differ nothing but in their names. Aldrovandus says, they be of a Trout kind; and Gesner says, that in his country, which is Switzerland, he is accounted the choicest of all fish. And in Italy, he is, in the month of May, so highly valued, that he is sold there at a much higher rate than any other fish. The French, which call the Chub Un Villain, call the Umber of the lake Leman Un Umble Chevalier; and they value the Umber or Grayling so highly, that they say he feeds on gold; and say, that many have been caught out of their famous river of Loire, out of whose bellies grains of gold have been often taken. And some think that he feeds on water thyme, and smells of it at his first taking out of the water; and they may think so with as good reason as we do that our Smelts smell like violets at their being first caught, which I think is a truth. Aldrovandus says, the Salmon, the Grayling, and Trout, and all fish that live in clear and sharp streams, are made by their mother Nature of such exact shape and pleasant colours purposely to invite us to a joy and contentedness in feasting with her. Whether this is a truth or not, is not my purpose to dispute: but 'tis certain, all that write of the Umber declare him to be very medicinable. And Gesner says, that the fat of an Umber or Grayling, being set, with a little honey, a day or two in the sun, in a little glass, is very excellent against redness or swarthiness, or anything that breeds in the eyes. Salvian takes him to be called Umber from his swift swimming, or gliding out of sight more like a shadow or a ghost than a fish. Much more might be said both of his smell and taste: but I shall only tell you that St. Ambrose, the glorious bishop of Milan, who lived when the church kept fasting-days, calls him the flower-fish, or flower of fishes; and that he was so far in love with him, that he would not let him pass without the honour of a long discourse; but I must; and pass on to tell you how to take this dainty fish.

First note, that he grows not to the bigness of a Trout; for the biggest of them do not usually exceed eighteen inches. He lives in such rivers as the Trout does; and is usually taken with the same baits as the Trout is, and after the same manner; for he will bite both at the minnow, or worm, or fly, though he bites not often at the minnow, and is very gamesome at the fly; and much simpler, and therefore bolder than a Trout; for he will rise twenty times at a fly, if you miss him, and yet rise again. He has been taken with a fly made of the red feathers of a paroquet, a strange outlandish bird; and he will rise at a fly not unlike a gnat, or a small moth, or, indeed, at most flies that are not too big. He is a fish that lurks close all Winter, but is very pleasant and jolly after mid-April, and in May, and in the hot months. He is of a very fine shape, his flesh is white, his teeth, those little ones that he has, are in his throat, yet he has so tender a mouth, that he is oftener lost after an angler has hooked him than any other fish. Though there be many of these fishes in the delicate river Dove, and in Trent, and some other smaller rivers, as that which runs by Salisbury, yet he is not so general a fish as the Trout, nor to me so good to eat or to angle for. And so I shall take my leave of him: and now come to some observations of the Salmon, and how to catch him.

## THE FOURTH DAY—*continued*

### *The Salmon*

### CHAPTER VII

PISCATOR

THE Salmon is accounted the King of freshwater fish; and is ever bred in rivers relating to the sea, yet so high, or far from it, as admits of no tincture of salt, or brackishness. He is said to breed or cast his spawn, in most rivers, in the month of August: some say, that then they dig a hole or grave in a safe place in the gravel, and there place their eggs or spawn, after the melter has done his natural office, and then hide it most cunningly, and cover it over with gravel and stones; and then leave it to their Creator's protection, who, by a gentle heat which he infuses into that cold element, makes it brood, and beget life in the spawn, and to become Samlets early in the spring next following.

The Salmons having spent their appointed time, and done this natural duty in the fresh waters, they then haste to the sea before winter, both the melter and spawner; but if they be stopt by flood-gates or weirs, or lost in the fresh waters, then those so left behind by degrees grow sick and lean, and unseasonable, and kipper, that is to say, have bony gristles grow out of their lower chaps, not unlike a hawk's beak, which hinders their feeding; and, in time, such fish so left behind pine away and die. 'Tis observed, that he may live thus one year from the sea; but he then grows insipid and tasteless, and loses both his blood and strength, and pines and dies the second year. And 'tis noted, that those little Salmons called Skeggers, which abound in many rivers relating to the sea, are bred by such sick Salmons that might not go to the sea, and that though they abound, yet they never thrive to any considerable bigness.

But if the old Salmon gets to the sea, then that gristle which shews him to be kipper, wears away, or is cast off, as the eagle is said to cast his bill, and he recovers his strength, and comes next summer to the same river, if it be possible, to enjoy the former pleasures that there possest him; for, as one has wittily observed, he has, like some persons of honour and riches which have both their winter and summer houses, the fresh rivers for summer, and the salt water for winter, to spend his life in; which is not, as Sir Francis Bacon hath observed in his *History of Life and Death,* above ten years. And it is to be observed, that though the Salmon does grow big in the sea, yet he grows not fat but in fresh rivers; and it is observed, that the farther they get from the sea, they be both the fatter and better.

Next, I shall tell you, that though they make very hard shift to get out of the fresh rivers into the sea, yet they will make harder shift to get out of the salt into the fresh rivers, to spawn, or possess the pleasures that they have formerly found in them: to which end, they will force themselves through floodgates, or over weirs, or hedges, or stops in the water, even to a height beyond common belief. Gesner speaks of such places as are known to be above eight feet high above water. And our Camden mentions, in his *Britannia,* the like wonder to be in Pembrokeshire, where the river Tivy falls into the sea; and that the fall is so downright, and so high, that the people stand and wonder at the strength and sleight by which they see the Salmon use to get out of the sea into the said river; and the manner and height of the place is so notable, that it is known, far, by the name of the Salmon-leap. Concerning which, take this also out of Michael Drayton, my honest old friend; as he tells it you, in his *Polyolbion:*

> And when the Salmon seeks a fresher stream to find;
> (Which hither from the sea comes, yearly, by his kind,)
> As he towards season grows; and stems the watry tract
> Where *Tivy,* falling down, makes an high cataract,
> Forc'd by the rising rocks that there her course oppose,
> As tho' within her bounds they meant her to inclose;
> Here when the labouring fish does at the foot arrive,
> And finds that by his strength he does but vainly strive;
> His tail takes in his mouth, and, bending like a bow
> That's to full compass drawn, aloft himself doth throw,
> Then springing at his height, as doth a little wand
> That bended end to end, and started from man's hand,
> Far off itself doth cast; so does that Salmon vault:
> And if, at first, he fail, his second summersault
> He instantly essays, and, from his nimble ring
> Still yerking, never leaves until himself he fling
> Above the opposing stream.

This Michael Drayton tells you, of this leap or summersault of the Salmon.

And, next, I shall tell you, that it is observed by Gesner and others, that there is no better Salmon than in England; and that though some of our northern counties have as fat, and as large, as the river Thames, yet none are of so excellent a taste.

And as I have told you that Sir Francis Bacon observes, the age of a Salmon exceeds not ten years; so let me next tell you, that his growth is very sudden: it is said, that after he is got into the sea, he becomes, from a Samlet not so big as a Gudgeon, to be a Salmon, in as short a time as a gosling becomes to be a goose. Much of this has been observed, by tying a riband, or some known tape or thread, in the tail of some young Salmons which have been taken in weirs as they have swimmed towards the salt water; and then by taking a part of them again, with the known mark, at the same place, at their return from the sea, which is usually about six months after; and the like experiment hath been tried upon young swallows, who have, after six months' absence, been observed to return to the same chimney, there to make their nests and habitations for the summer following; which has inclined many to think, that every Salmon usually returns to the same river in which it was bred, as young pigeons taken out of the same dovecote have also been observed to do.

And you are yet to observe further, that the He-salmon is usually bigger than the Spawner; and that he is more kipper, and less able to endure a winter in the fresh water than the She is: yet she is, at that time of looking less kipper and better, as watry, and as bad meat.

And yet you are to observe, that as there is no general rule without an exception, so there are some few rivers in this nation that have Trouts and Salmon in season in winter, as 'tis certain there be in the river Wye in Monmouthshire, where they be in season, as Camden observes, from September till April. But, my scholar, the observation of this and many other things I must in manners omit, because they will prove too large for our narrow compass of time, and, therefore, I shall next fall upon my directions how to fish for this Salmon.

And, for that: First you shall observe, that usually he stays not long in a place, as Trouts will, but, as I said, covets still to go nearer the spring-head: and that he does not, as the Trout and many other fish, lie near the water-side or bank, or roots of trees, but swims in the deep and broad parts of the water, and usually in the middle, and near the ground, and that there you are to fish for him, and that he is to be caught, as the Trout is, with a worm, a minnow which some call a penk, or with a fly.

And you are to observe, that he is very seldom observed to bite at a minnow, yet sometimes he will, and not usually at a fly, but more usually at a worm, and then most usually at a lob or garden-worm, which should be well scoured, that is to say, kept seven or eight days in moss before you fish with them: and if you double your time of eight into sixteen, twenty, or more days, it is still the better; for the worms will still be clearer, tougher, and more lively, and continue so longer upon your hook. And they may be kept longer by keeping them cool, and in fresh moss; and some advise to put camphire into it.

Note also, that many used to fish for a Salmon with a ring of wire on the top of their rod, through which the line may run to as great a length as is needful, when he is hooked. And to that end, some use a wheel about the middle of their rod, or near their hand, which is to be observed better by seeing one of them than by a large demonstration of words.

And now I shall tell you that which may be called a secret. I have been a-fishing with old Oliver Henly, now with God, a noted fisher both for Trout and Salmon; and have observed, that he would usually take three or four worms out of his bag, and put them into a little box in his pocket, where he would usually let them continue half an hour or more, before he would bait his hook with them. I have asked him his reason, and he has replied, "He did but pick the best out to be in readiness against he baited his hook the next time": but he has been observed, both by others and myself, to catch more fish than I, or any other body that has ever gone a-fishing with him, could do, and especially Salmons. And I have been told lately, by one of his most intimate and secret friends, that the box in which he put those worms was anointed with a drop, or two or three, of the oil of ivy-berries, made by expression or infusion; and told, that by the worms remaining in that box an hour, or a like time, they had incorporated a kind of smell that was irresistibly attractive, enough to force any fish within the smell of them to bite. This I heard not long since from a friend, but have not tried it; yet I grant it probable, and refer my reader to Sir Francis Bacon's *Natural History*, where he proves fishes may hear, and, doubtless, can more probably smell: and I am certain Gesner says, the Otter can smell in the water; and I know not but that fish may do so too. 'Tis left for a lover of angling, or any that desires to improve that art, to try this conclusion.

I shall also impart two other experiments, but not tried by myself, which I will deliver in the same words that they were given me by an excellent angler and a very friend, in writing: he told me the latter was too good to be told, but in a learned language, lest it should be made common.

"Take the stinking oil drawn out of polypody of the oak by a retort, mixed with turpentine and hive-honey, and anoint your bait therewith, and it will doubtless draw the fish to it." The other is this: "Vulnera hederæ grandissimæ inflicta sudant balsamum oleo gelato, albicantique persimile, odoris verò longè suavissimi." "'Tis supremely sweet to any fish, and yet assa fœtida may do the like."

But in these I have no great faith; yet grant it probable; and have had from some chymical men, namely, from Sir George Hastings and others, an affirmation of them to be very advantageous. But no more of these; especially not in this place.

I might here, before I take my leave of the Salmon, tell you, that there is more than one sort of them, as namely, a Tecon, and another called in some places a Samlet, or by some a Skegger; but these, and others which I forbear to name, may be fish of another kind, and differ as we know a Herring and a Pilchard do, which, I think, are as different as the rivers in which they breed, and must, by me, be left to the disquisitions of men of more leisure, and of greater abilities than I profess myself to have.

And lastly, I am to borrow so much of your promised patience, as to tell you, that the trout, or Salmon, being in season, have, at their first taking out of the water, which continues during life, their bodies adorned, the one with such red spots, and the other with such black or blackish spots, as give them such an addition of natural beauty as, I think, was never given to any woman by the artificial paint or patches in which they so much pride themselves in this age. And so I shall leave them both; and proceed to some observations of the Pike.

# THE FOURTH DAY—*continued*

## *On the Luce or Pike*

### CHAPTER VIII

#### PISCATOR AND VENATOR

PISCATOR. The mighty Luce or Pike is taken to be the tyrant, as the Salmon is the king, of the fresh water. 'Tis not to be doubted, but that they are bred, some by generation, and some not; as namely, of a weed called pickerel-weed, unless learned Gesner be much mistaken, for he says, this weed and other glutinous matter, with the help of the sun's heat, in some particular months, and some ponds, apted for it by nature, do become Pikes. But, doubtless, divers Pikes are bred after this manner, or are brought into some ponds some such other ways as is past man's finding out, of which we have daily testimonies.

Sir Francis Bacon, in his *History of Life and Death*, observes the Pike to be the longest lived of any fresh-water fish; and yet he computes it to be not usually above forty years; and others think it to be not above ten years: and yet Gesner mentions a Pike taken in Swedeland, in the year 1449, with a ring about his neck, declaring he was put into that pond by Frederick the Second, more than two hundred years before he was last taken, as by the inscription in that ring, being Greek, was interpreted by the then Bishop of Worms. But of this no more; but that it is observed, that the old or very great Pikes have in them more of state than goodness; the smaller or middle-sized Pikes being, by the most and choicest palates, observed to be the best meat: and, contrary, the Eel is observed to be the better for age and bigness.

All Pikes that live long prove chargeable to their keepers, because their life is maintained by the death of so many other fish, even those of their own kind; which has made him by some writers to be called the tyrant of the rivers, or the fresh-water wolf, by reason of his bold, greedy, devouring, disposition; which is so keen, as Gesner relates, A man going to a pond, where it seems a Pike had devoured all the fish, to water his mule, had a Pike bit his mule by the lips; to which the Pike hung so fast, that the mule drew him out of the water; and by that accident, the owner of the mule angled out the Pike. And the same Gesner observes, that a maid in Poland had a Pike bit her by the foot, as she was washing clothes in a pond. And I have heard the like of a woman in Killingworth pond, not far from Coventry. But I have been assured by my friend Mr. Segrave, of whom I spake to you formerly, that keeps tame Otters, that he hath known a Pike, in extreme hunger, fight with one of his Otters for a Carp that the Otter had caught, and was then bringing out of the water. I have told you who relate these things; and tell you they are persons of credit; and shall conclude this observation, by telling you, what a wise man has observed, "It is a hard thing to persuade the belly, because it has no ears."

But if these relations be disbelieved, it is too evident to be doubted, that a Pike will devour a fish of his own kind that shall be bigger than his belly or throat will receive, and swallow a part of him, and let the other part remain in his mouth till the swallowed part be digested, and then swallow that other part that was in his mouth, and so put it over by degrees; which is not unlike the Ox, and some other beasts taking their meat, not out of their mouth immediately into their belly, but first into some place betwixt, and then chew it, or digest it by degrees after, which is called chewing the cud. And, doubtless, Pikes will bite when they are not hungry; but, as some think, even for very anger, when a tempting bait comes near to them.

And it is observed, that the Pike will eat venomous things, as some kind of frogs are, and yet live without being harmed by them; for, as some say, he has in him a natural balsam, or antidote against all poison. And he has a strange heat, that though it appear to us to be cold, can yet digest or put over any fish-flesh, by degrees, without being sick. And others observe, that he never eats the venomous frog till he have first killed her, and then as ducks are observed to do to frogs in spawning-time, at which time some frogs are observed to be venomous, so thoroughly washed her, by tumbling her up and down in the water, that he may devour her without danger. And Gesner affirms, that a Polonian gentleman did faithfully assure him, he had seen two young geese at one time in the belly of a Pike. And doubtless a Pike in his height of hunger will bite at and devour a dog that swims in a pond; and there have been examples of it, or the like; for as I told you, "The belly has no ears when hunger comes upon it."

The Pike is also observed to be a solitary, melancholy, and a bold fish; melancholy, because he always swims or rests himself alone, and never swims in shoals or with company, as Roach and Dace, and most other fish do: and bold, because he fears not a shadow, or to see or be seen of anybody, as the Trout and Chub, and all other fish do.

And it is observed by Gesner, that the jaw-bones, and hearts, and galls of Pikes, are very medicinable for several diseases, or to stop blood, to abate fevers, to cure agues, to oppose or expel the infection of the plague, and to be many ways medicinable and useful for the good of mankind: but he observes, that the biting of a Pike is venomous, and hard to be cured.

And it is observed, that the Pike is a fish that breeds but once a year; and that other fish, as namely Loaches, do breed oftener: as we are certain tame Pigeons do almost every month; and yet the Hawk, a bird of prey, as the Pike is a fish, breeds but once in twelve months. And you are to note, that his time of breeding, or spawning, is usually about the end of February, or, somewhat later, in March, as the weather proves colder or warmer: and to note, that his manner of breeding is thus: a he and a she Pike will usually go together out of a river into some ditch or creek; and that there the spawner casts her eggs, and the melter hovers over her all that time that she is casting her spawn, but touches her not.

I might say more of this, but it might be thought curiosity or worse, and shall therefore forbear it; and take up so much of your attention as to tell you that the best of Pikes are noted to be in rivers; next, those in great ponds or meres; and the worst, in small ponds.

But before I proceed further, I am to tell you, that there is a great antipathy betwixt the Pike and some frogs: and this may appear to the reader of Dubravius, a bishop in Bohemia, who, in his book *Of Fish and Fish-ponds*, relates what he says he saw with his own eyes, and could not forbear to tell the reader. Which was:

"As he and the bishop Thurzo were walking by a large pond in Bohemia, they saw a frog, when the Pike lay very sleepily and quiet by the shore side, leap upon his head; and the frog having expressed malice or anger by his swoln cheeks and staring eyes, did stretch out his legs and embrace the Pike's head, and presently reached them to his eyes, tearing with them, and his teeth, those tender parts: the Pike, moved with anguish, moves up and down the water, and rubs himself against weeds, and whatever he thought might quit him of his enemy; but all in vain, for the frog did continue to ride triumphantly, and to bite and torment the Pike till his strength failed; and then the frog sunk with the Pike to the bottom of the water: then presently the frog appeared again at the top, and croaked, and seemed to rejoice like a conqueror, after which he presently retired to his secret hole. The bishop, that had beheld the battle, called his fisherman to fetch his nets, and by all means to get the Pike that they might declare what had happened: and the Pike was drawn forth, and both his eyes eaten out; at which when they began to wonder, the fisherman wished them to forbear, and assured them he was certain that Pikes were often so served."

I told this, which is to be read in the sixth chapter of the book of Dubravius, unto a friend, who replied, "It was as improbable as to have the mouse scratch out the cat's eyes." But he did not consider, that there be Fishing frogs, which the Dalmatians call the Water-devil, of which I might tell you as wonderful a story: but I shall tell you that 'tis not to be doubted but that there be some frogs so fearful of the water-snake, that when they swim in a place in which they fear to meet with him they then get a reed across into their mouths; which if they two meet by accident, secures the frog from the strength and malice of the snake; and note, that the frog usually swims the fastest of the two.

And let me tell you, that as there be water and land frogs, so there be land and water snakes. Concerning which take this observation, that the land-snake breeds and hatches her eggs, which become young snakes, in some old dunghill, or a like hot place: but the water-snake, which is not venomous, and as I have been assured by a great observer of such secrets, does not hatch, but breed her young alive, which she does not then forsake, but bides with them, and in case of danger will take them all into her mouth and swim away from any apprehended danger, and then let them out again when she thinks all danger to be past: these be accidents that we Anglers sometimes see, and often talk of.

But whither am I going? I had almost lost myself, by remembering the discourse of Dubravius. I will therefore stop here; and tell you, according to my promise, how to catch this Pike.

His feeding is usually of fish or frogs; and sometimes a weed of his own, called pickerel-weed, of which I told you some think Pikes are bred; for they have observed, that where none have been put into ponds, yet they have there found many; and that there has been plenty of that weed in those ponds, and that that weed both breeds and feeds them: but whether those Pikes, so bred, will ever breed by generation as the others do, I shall leave to the disquisitions of men of more curiosity and leisure than I profess myself to have: and shall proceed to tell you, that you may fish for a Pike, either with a ledger or a walking-bait; and you are to note, that I call that a Ledger-bait, which is fixed or made to rest in one certain place when you shall be absent from it; and I call that a Walking-bait, which you take with you, and have ever in motion. Concerning which two, I shall give you this direction; that your ledger-bait is best to be a living bait (though a dead one may catch), whether it be a fish or a frog: and that you may make them live the longer, you may, or indeed you must, take this course:

First, for your LIVE-BAIT. Of fish, a roach or dace is, I think, best and most tempting; and a perch is the longest lived on a hook, and having cut off his fin on his back, which may be done without hurting him, you must take your knife, which cannot be too sharp, and betwixt the head and the fin on the back, cut or make an incision, or such a scar, as you may put the arming-wire of your hook into it, with as little bruising or hurting the fish as art and diligence will enable you to do; and so carrying your arming-wire along his back, unto or near the tail of your fish, betwixt the skin and the body of it, draw out that wire or arming of your hook at another scar near to his tail: then tie him about it with thread, but no harder than of necessity, to prevent hurting the fish; and the better to avoid hurting the fish, some have a kind of probe to open the way for the more easy entrance and passage of your wire or arming: but as for these, time and a little experience will teach you better than I can by words. Therefore I will for the present say no more of this; but come next to give you some directions how to bait your hook with a frog.

VENATOR. But, good master, did you not say even now, that some frogs were venomous; and is it not dangerous to touch them?

PISCATOR. Yes, but I will give you some rules or cautions concerning them. And first you are to note, that there are two kinds of frogs, that is to say, if I may so express myself, a flesh and fish frog. By flesh-frogs, I mean frogs that breed and live on the land; and of these there be several sorts also, and of several colours, some being speckled, some greenish, some blackish, or brown: the green frog, which is a small one, is, by Topsel, taken to be venomous; and so is the paddock, or frog-paddock, which usually keeps or breeds on the land, and is very large and bony, and big, especially the she-frog of that kind: yet these will sometimes come into the water, but it is not often: and the land-frogs are some of them observed by him, to breed by laying eggs; and others to breed of the slime and dust of the earth, and that in winter they turn to slime again, and that the next summer that very slime returns to be a living creature; this is the opinion of Pliny. And Cardanus undertakes to give a reason for the raining of frogs: but if it were in my power, it should rain none but water-frogs; for those I think are not venomous, especially the right water-frog, which, about February or March, breeds in ditches, by slime, and blackish eggs in that slime: about which time of breeding, the he and she frogs are observed to use divers summersaults, and to croak and make a noise, which the land-frog, or paddock-frog, never does.

Now of these water-frogs, if you intend to fish with a frog for a Pike, you are to choose the yellowest that you can get, for that the Pike ever likes best. And thus use your frog, that he may continue long alive:

Put your hook into his mouth, which you may easily do from the middle of April till August; and then the frog's mouth grows up, and he continues so for at least six months without eating, but is sustained, none but He whose name is Wonderful knows how: I say, put your hook, I mean the arming-wire, through his mouth, and out at his gills; and then with a fine needle and silk sew the upper part of his leg, with only one stitch, to the arming-wire of your hook; or tie the frog's leg, above the upper joint, to the armed-wire; and, in so doing, use him as though you loved him, that is, harm him as little as you may possibly, that he may live the longer.

And now, having given you this direction for the baiting your ledger-hook with a live fish or frog, my next must be to tell you, how your hook thus baited must or may be used; and it is thus: having fastened your hook to a line, which if it be not fourteen yards long should not be less than twelve, you are to fasten that line to any bough near to a hole where a Pike is, or is likely to lie, or to have a haunt; and then wind your line on any forked stick, all your line, except half a yard of it or rather more; and split that forked stick, with such a nick or notch at one end of it as may keep the line from any more of it ravelling from about the stick than so much of it as you intend. And choose your forked stick to be of that bigness as may keep the fish or frog from pulling the forked stick under the water till the Pike bites; and then the Pike having pulled the line forth of the cleft or nick of that stick in which it was gently fastened, he will have line enough to go to his hold and pouch the bait. And if you would have this ledger-bait to keep at a fixt place undisturbed by wind or other accidents which may drive it to the shore-side, for you are to note, that it is likeliest to catch a Pike in the midst of the water, then hang a small plummet of lead, a stone, or piece of tile, or a turf, in a string, and cast it into the water with the forked stick to hang upon the ground, to be a kind of anchor to keep the forked stick from moving out of your intended place till the Pike come: this I take to be a very good way to use so many ledger-baits as you intend to make trial of.

Or if you bait your hooks thus with live fish or frogs, and in a windy day, fasten them thus to a bough or bundle of straw, and by the help of that wind can get them to move across a pond or mere, you are like to stand still on the shore and see sport presently, if there be any store of Pikes. Or these live baits may make sport, being tied about the body or wings of a goose or duck, and she chased over a pond. And the like may be done with turning three or four live baits, thus fastened to bladders, or boughs, or bottles of hay or flags, to swim down a river, whilst you walk quietly alone on the shore, and are still in expectaion of sport. The rest must be taught you by practice; for time will not allow me to say more of this kind of fishing with live baits.

And for your DEAD-BAIT for a Pike: for that you may be taught by one day's going a-fishing with me, or any other body that fishes for him; for the baiting your hook with a dead gudgeon or a roach, and moving it up and down the water, is too easy a thing to take up any time to direct you to do it. And yet, because I cut you short in that, I will commute for it by telling you that that was told me for a secret: it is this: Dissolve gum of ivy in oil of spike, and therewith anoint your dead bait for a Pike; and then cast it into a likely place; and when it has lain a short time at the bottom, draw it towards the top of the water, and so up the stream; and it is more than likely that you have a Pike follow with more than common eagerness. And some affirm, that any bait anointed with the marrow of the thigh-bone of a heron is a great temptation to any fish.

These have not been tried by me, but told me by a friend of note, that pretended to do me a courtesy. But if this direction to catch a Pike thus do you no good, yet I am certain this direction how to roast him when he is caught is choicely good; for I have tried it, and it is somewhat the better for not being common. But with my direction you must take this caution, that your Pike must not be a small one, that is, it must be more than half a yard, and should be bigger.

"First, open your Pike at the gills, and if need be, cut also a little slit towards the belly. Out of these, take his guts; and keep his liver, which you are to shred very small, with thyme, sweet marjoram, and a little winter-savoury; to these put some pickled oysters, and some anchovies, two or three; both these last whole, for the anchovies will melt, and the oysters should not; to these, you must add also a pound of sweet butter, which you are to mix with the herbs that are shred, and let them all be well salted. If the Pike be more than a yard long, then you may put into these herbs more than a pound, or if he be less, then less butter will suffice: These, being thus mixt, with a blade or two of mace, must be put into the Pike's belly; and then his belly so sewed up as to keep all the butter in his belly if it be possible; if not, then as much of it as you possibly can. But take not off the scales. Then you are to thrust the spit through his mouth, out at his tail. And then take four or five or six split sticks, or very thin laths, and a convenient quantity of tape or filleting; these laths are to be tied round about the Pike's body, from his head to his tail, and the tape tied somewhat thick, to prevent his breaking or falling off from the spit. Let him be roasted very leisurely; and often basted with claret wine, and anchovies, and butter, mixt together; and also with what moisture falls from him into the pan. When you have roasted him sufficiently, you are to hold under him, when you unwind or cut the tape that ties him, such a dish as you purpose to eat him out of; and let him fall into it with the sauce that is roasted in his belly; and by this means the Pike will be kept unbroken and complete. Then, to the sauce which was within, and also that sauce in the pan, you are to add a fit quantity of the best butter, and to squeeze the juice of three or four oranges. Lastly, you may either put it into the Pike, with the oysters, two cloves of garlick, and take it whole out, when the Pike is cut off the spit; or, to give the sauce a haut goût, let the dish into which you let the Pike fall be rubbed with it: The using or not using of this garlick is left to your discretion. M. B."

This dish of meat is too good for any but anglers, or very honest men; and I trust you will prove both, and therefore I have trusted you with this secret.

Let me next tell you, that Gesner tells us, there are no Pikes in Spain, and that the largest are in the lake Thrasymene in Italy; and the next, if not equal to them, are the Pikes of England; and that in England, Lincolnshire boasteth to have the biggest. Just so doth Sussex boast of four sorts of fish, namely, an Arundel Mullet, a Chichester Lobster, a Shelsey Cockle, and an Amerly Trout.

But I will take up no more of your time with this relation, but proceed to give you some Observations of the Carp, and how to angle for him; and to dress him but not till he is caught.

# THE FOURTH DAY—*continued*

## *On the Carp*

### CHAPTER IX

PISCATOR

THE Carp is the queen of rivers; a stately, a good, and a very subtil fish; that was not at first bred, nor hath been long in England, but is now naturalised. It is said, they were brought hither by one Mr. Mascal, a gentleman that then lived at Plumsted in Sussex, a county that abounds more with this fish than any in this nation.

You may remember that I told you Gesner says there are no Pikes in Spain; and doubtless there was a time, about a hundred or a few more years ago, when there were no Carps in England, as may seem to be affirmed by Sir Richard Baker, in whose Chronicle you may find these verses:

> Hops and turkies, carps and beer,
> Came into England all in a year.

And doubtless, as of sea-fish the Herring dies soonest out of the water, and of fresh-water fish the Trout, so, except the Eel, the Carp endures most hardness, and lives longest out of its own proper element; and, therefore, the report of the Carp's being brought out of a foreign country into this nation is the more probable.

Carps and Loaches are observed to breed several months in one year, which Pikes and most other fish do not; and this is partly proved by tame and wild rabbits; as also by some ducks, which will lay eggs nine of the twelve months; and yet there be other ducks that lay not longer than about one month. And it is the rather to be believed, because you shall scarce or never take a male Carp without a melt, or a female without a roe or spawn, and for the most part very much, and especially all the summer season; and it is observed, that they breed more naturally in ponds than in running waters, if they breed there at all; and that those that live in rivers are taken by men of the best palates to be much the better meat.

And it is observed that in some ponds Carps will not breed, especially in cold ponds; but where they will breed, they breed innumerably: Aristotle and Pliny say, six times in a year, if there be no Pikes nor Perch to devour their spawn, when it is cast upon grass or flags, or weeds, where it lies ten or twelve days before it be enlivened.

The Carp, if he have water-room and good feed, will grow to a very great bigness and length; I have heard, to be much above a yard long. It is said by Jovius, who hath writ of fishes, that in the lake Lurian in Italy, Carps have thriven to be more than fifty pounds weight: which is the more probable, for as the bear is conceived and born suddenly, and being born is but short lived; so, on the contrary, the elephant is said to be two years in his dam's belly, some think he is ten years in it, and being born, grows in bigness twenty years; and it is observed too, that he lives to the age of a hundred years. And 'tis also observed, that the crocodile is very long-lived; and more than that, that all that long life he thrives in bigness; and so I think some Carps do, especially in some places, though I never saw one above twenty-three inches, which was a great and goodly fish; but have been assured there are of a far greater size, and in England too.

Now, as the increase of Carps is wonderful for their number, so there is not a reason found out, I think, by any, why they should breed in some ponds, and not in others, of the same nature for soil and all other circumstances. And as their breeding, so are their decays also very mysterious: I have both read it, and been told by a gentleman of tried honesty, that he has known sixty or more large Carps put into several ponds near to a house, where, by reason of the stakes in the ponds, and the owner's constant being near to them, it was impossible they should be stole away from him; and that when he has, after three or four years, emptied the pond, and expected an increase from them by breeding young ones, for that they might do so he had, as the rule is, put in three melters for one spawner, he has, I say, after three or four years, found neither a young nor old Carp remaining. And the like I have known of one that had almost watched the pond, and, at a like distance of time, at the fishing of a pond, found, of seventy or eighty large Carps, not above five or six: and that he had forborne longer to fish the said pond, but that he saw, in a hot day in summer, a large Carp swim near the top of the water with a frog upon his head; and that he, upon that occasion, caused his pond to be let dry: and I say, of seventy or eighty Carps, only found five or six in the said pond, and those very sick and lean, and with every one a frog sticking so fast on the head of the said Carps, that the frog would not be got off without extreme force or killing. And the gentleman that did affirm this to me, told me he saw it; and did declare his belief to be, and I also believe the same, that he thought the other

Carps, that were so strangely lost, were so killed by the frogs, and then devoured.

And a person of honour, now living in Worcestershire, assured me he had seen a necklace, or collar of tadpoles, hang like a chain or necklace of beads about a Pike's neck, and to kill him: Whether it were for meat or malice, must be, to me, a question.

But I am fallen into this discourse by accident; of which I might say more, but it has proved longer than I intended, and possibly may not to you be considerable: I shall therefore give you three or four more short observations of the Carp, and then fall upon some directions how you shall fish for him.

The age of Carps is by Sir Francis Bacon, in his *History of Life and Death*, observed to be but ten years; yet others think they live longer. Gesner says, a Carp has been known to live in the Palatine above a hundred years. But most conclude, that, contrary to the Pike or Luce, all Carps are the better for age and bigness. The tongues of Carps are noted to be choice and costly meat, especially to them that buy them: but Gesner says, Carps have no tongue like other fish, but a piece of fleshlike fish in their mouth like to a tongue, and should be called a palate: but it is certain it is choicely good, and that the Carp is to be reckoned amongst those leather-mouthed fish which, I told you, have their teeth in their throat; and for that reason he is very seldom lost by breaking his hold, if your hook be once stuck into his chaps.

I told you that Sir Francis Bacon thinks that the Carp lives but ten years: but Janus Dubravius has writ a book *Of fish and fish-ponds* in which he says, that Carps begin to spawn at the age of three years, and continue to do so till thirty: he says also, that in the time of their breeding, which is in summer, when the sun hath warmed both the earth and water, and so apted them also for generation, that then three or four male Carps will follow a female; and that then, she putting on a seeming coyness, they force her through weeds and flags, where she lets fall her eggs or spawn, which sticks fast to the weeds; and then they let fall their melt upon it, and so it becomes in a short time to be a living fish: and, as I told you, it is thought that the Carp does this several months in the year; and most believe, that most fish breed after this manner, except the Eel. And it has been observed, that when the spawner has weakened herself by doing that natural office, that two or three melters have helped her from off the weeds, by bearing her up on both sides, and guarding her into the deep. And you may note, that though this may seem a curiosity not worth observing, yet others have judged it worth their time and costs to make glass hives, and order them in such a manner as to see how bees have bred and made their honeycombs, and how they have obeyed their king, and governed their commonwealth. But it is thought that all Carps are not bred by generation; but that some breed other ways, as some Pikes do.

The physicians make the galls and stones in the heads of Carps to be very medicinable. But it is not to be doubted but that in Italy they make great profit of the spawn of Carps, by selling it to the Jews, who make it into red caviare; the Jews not being by their law admitted to eat of caviare made of the Sturgeon, that being a fish that wants scales, and, as may appear in Leviticus xi., by them reputed to be unclean.

Much more might be said out of him, and out of Aristotle, which Dubravius often quotes in his *Discourse of Fishes:* but it might rather perplex than satisfy you; and therefore I shall rather choose to direct you how to catch, than spend more time in discoursing either of the nature or the breeding of this Carp, or of any more circumstances concerning him. But yet I shall remember you of what I told you before, that he is a very subtil fish, and hard to be caught.

And my first direction is, that if you will fish for a Carp, you must put on a very large measure of patience, especially to fish for a river Carp: I have known a very good fisher angle diligently four or six hours in a day, for three or four days together, for a river Carp, and not have a bite. And you are to note, that, in some ponds, it is as hard to catch a Carp as in a river; that is to say, where they have store of feed, and the water is of a clayish colour. But you are to remember that I have told you there is no rule without an exception; and therefore being possest with that hope and patience which I wish to all fishers, especially to the Carp-angler, I shall tell you with what bait to fish for him. But first you are to know, that it must be either early, or late; and let me tell you, that in hot weather, for he will seldom bite in cold, you cannot be too early, or too late at it. And some have been so curious as to say, the tenth of April is a fatal day for Carps.

The Carp bites either at worms, or at paste: and of worms I think the bluish marsh or meadow worm is best; but possibly another worm, not too big, may do as well, and so may a green gentle: and as for pastes, there are almost as many sorts as there are medicines for the toothache; but doubtless sweet pastes are best; I mean, pastes made with honey or with sugar: which, that you may the better beguile this crafty fish, should be thrown into the pond or place in which you fish for him, some hours, or longer, before you undertake your trial of skill with the angle-rod; and doubtless, if it be thrown into the water a day or two before, at several times, and in small pellets, you are the likelier, when you fish for the Carp, to obtain your desired sport. Or, in a large pond, to draw them to any certain place, that they may the better and with more hope be fished for, you are to throw into it, in some certain place, either grains, or blood mixt with cow-dung or with bran; or any garbage, as chicken's guts or the like; and then, some of your small sweet pellets with which you propose to angle: and these small pellets being a few of them also thrown in as you are angling, will be the better.

And your paste must be thus made: take the flesh of a rabbit, or cat, cut small; and bean-flour; and if that may not be easily got, get other flour; and then, mix these together, and put to them either sugar, or honey, which I think better: and then beat these together in a mortar, or sometimes work them in your hands, your hands being very clean; and then make it into a ball, or two, or three, as you like best, for your use: but you must work or pound it so long in the mortar, as to make it so tough as to hang upon your hook without washing from it, yet not too hard: or, that you may the better keep it on your hook, you may knead with your paste a little, and not too much, white or yellowish wool.

And if you would have this paste keep all the year, for any other fish, then mix with it virgin-wax and clarified honey, and work them together with your hands, before the fire; then make these into balls, and they will keep all the year.

And if you fish for a Carp with gentles, then put upon your hook a small piece of scarlet about this bigness □, it being soaked in or anointed with oil of petre, called by some, oil of the rock: and if your gentles be put, two or three days before, into a box or horn anointed with honey, and so put upon your hook as to preserve them to be living, you are as like to kill this crafty fish this way as any other: but still, as you are fishing, chew a little white or brown bread in your mouth, and cast it into the pond about the place where your float swims. Other baits there be; but these, with diligence and patient watchfulness, will do better than any that I have ever practiced or heard of. And yet I shall tell you, that the crumbs of white bread and honey made into a paste is a good bait for a Carp; and you know, it is more easily made. And having said thus much of the Carp, my next discourse shall be of the Bream, which shall not prove so tedious; and therefore I desire the continuance of your attention.

But, first, I will tell you how to make this Carp, that is so curious to be caught, so curious a dish of meat as shall make him worth all your labour and patience. And though it is not without some trouble and charges, yet it will recompense both.

Take a Carp, alive if possible; scour him, and rub him clean with water and salt, but scale him not: then open him; and put him, with his blood and his liver, which you must save when you open him, into a small pot or kettle: then take sweet marjoram, thyme, and parsley, of each half a handful; a sprig of rosemary, and another of savoury; bind them into two or three small bundles, and put them in your Carp, with four or five whole onions, twenty pickled oysters, and three anchovies. Then pour upon your Carp as much claret wine as will only cover him; and season your claret well with salt, cloves, and mace, and the rinds of oranges and lemons. That done, cover your pot and set it on a quick fire till it be sufficiently boiled. Then take out the Carp; and lay it, with the broth, into the dish; and pour upon it a quarter of a pound of the best fresh butter, melted, and beaten with half a dozen spoonfuls of the broth, the yolks of two or three eggs, and some of the herbs shred: garnish your dish with lemons, and so serve it up. And much good do you! Dr. T.

# THE FOURTH DAY—*continued*

## *On the Bream*

## CHAPTER X

PISCATOR

THE Bream, being at a full growth, is a large and stately fish. He will breed both in rivers and ponds: but loves best to live in ponds, and where, if he likes the water and air, he will grow not only to be very large, but as fat as a hog. He is by Gesner taken to be more pleasant, or sweet, than wholesome. This fish is long in growing; but breeds exceedingly in a water that pleases him; yea, in many ponds so fast, as to overstore them, and starve the other fish.

He is very broad, with a forked tail, and his scales set in excellent order; he hath large eyes, and a narrow sucking mouth; he hath two sets of teeth, and a lozenge-like bone, a bone to help his grinding. The melter is observed to have two large melts; and the female, two large bags of eggs or spawn.

Gesner reports, that in Poland a certain and a great number of large breams were put into a pond, which in the next following winter were frozen up into one entire ice, and not one drop of water remaining, nor one of these fish to be found, though they were diligently searched for; and yet the next spring, when the ice was thawed, and the weather warm, and fresh water got into the pond, he affirms they all appeared again. This Gesner affirms; and I quote my author, because it seems almost as incredible as the resurrection to an atheist: but it may win something, in point of believing it, to him that considers the breeding or renovation of the silk-worm, and of many insects. And that is considerable, which Sir Francis Bacon observes in his *History of Life and Death*, fol. 20, that there be some herbs that die and spring every year, and some endure longer.

But though some do not, yet the French esteem this fish highly; and to that end have this proverb, "He that hath Breams in his pond, is able to bid his friend welcome"; and it is noted, that the best part of a Bream is his belly and head.

Some say, that Breams and Roaches will mix their eggs and melt together; and so there is in many places a bastard breed of Breams, that never come to be either large or good, but very numerous.

The baits good to catch this Bream are many. First, paste made of brown bread and honey; gentles; or the brood of wasps that be young, and then not unlike gentles, and should be hardened in an oven, or dried on a tile before the fire to make them tough. Or, there is, at the root of docks or flags or rushes, in watery places, a worm not unlike a maggot, at which Tench will bite freely. Or he will bite at a grasshopper with his legs nipt off, in June and July; or at several flies, under water, which may be found on flags that grow near to the water-side. I doubt not but that there be many other baits that are good; but I will turn them all into this most excellent one, either for a Carp or Bream, in any river or mere: it was given to me by a most honest and excellent angler; and hoping you will prove both, I will impart it to you.

1. Let your bait be as big a red worm as you can find, without a knot: get a pint or quart of them in an evening, in garden-walks, or chalky commons, after a shower of rain; and put them with clean moss well washed and picked, and the water squeezed out of the moss as dry as you can, into an earthen pot or pipkin set dry; and change the moss fresh every three or four days, for three weeks or a month together; then your bait will be at the best, for it will be clear and lively.

2. Having thus prepared your baits, get your tackling ready and fitted for this sport. Take three long angling-rods; and as many and more silk, or silk and hair, lines; and as many large swan or goose-quill floats. Then take a piece of lead, and fasten them to the low ends of your lines: then fasten your link-hook also to the lead; and let there be about a foot or ten inches between the lead and the hook: but be sure the lead be heavy enough to sink the float or quill, a little under the water; and not the quill to bear up the lead, for the lead must lie on the ground. Note, that your link next the hook may be smaller than the rest of your line, if you dare adventure, for fear of taking the Pike or Perch, who will assuredly visit your hooks, till they be taken out, as I will show you afterwards, before either Carp or Bream will come near to bite. Note also, that when the worm is well baited, it will crawl up and down as far as the lead will give leave, which much enticeth the fish to bite without suspicion.

3. Having thus prepared your baits, and fitted your tackling, repair to the river, where you have seen them swim in skulls or shoals, in the summer-time, in a hot afternoon, about three or four of the clock; and watch their going forth of their deep holes, and returning, which you may well discern, for they return about four of the clock, most of them seeking food at the bottom, yet one or two will lie on the top of the

water, rolling and tumbling themselves, whilst the rest are under him at the bottom; and so you shall perceive him to keep sentinel: then mark where he plays most and stays longest, which commonly is in the broadest and deepest place of the river; and there, or near thereabouts, at a clear bottom and a convenient landing-place, take one of your angles ready fitted as aforesaid, and sound the bottom, which should be about eight or ten feet deep; two yards from the bank is best. Then consider with yourself, whether that water will rise or fall by the next morning, by reason of any water-mills near; and, according to your discretion, take the depth of the place, where you mean after to cast your ground-bait, and to fish, to half an inch; that the lead lying on or near the ground-bait, the top of the float may only appear upright half an inch above the water.

Thus you having found and fitted for the place and depth thereof, then go home and prepare your ground-bait, which is, next to the fruit of your labours, to be regarded.

### THE GROUND-BAIT.

You shall take a peck, or a peck and a half, according to the greatness of the stream and deepness of the water, where you mean to angle, of sweet gross-ground barley-malt; and boil it in a kettle, one or two warms is enough: then strain it through a bag into a tub, the liquor whereof hath often done my horse much good; and when the bag and malt is near cold, take it down to the water-side, about eight or nine of the clock in the evening, and not before: cast in two parts of your ground-bait, squeezed hard between both your hands; it will sink presently to the bottom; and be sure it may rest in the very place where you mean to angle: if the stream run hard, or move a little, cast your malt in handfuls a little the higher, upwards the stream. You may, between your hands, close the malt so fast in handfuls, that the water will hardly part it with the fall.

Your ground thus baited, and tackling fitted, leave your bag, with the rest of your tackling and ground-bait, near the sporting-place all night; and in the morning, about three or four of the clock, visit the water-side, but not too near, for they have a cunning watchman, and are watchful themselves too.

Then, gently take one of your three rods, and bait your hook; casting it over your ground-bait, and gently and secretly draw it to you till the lead rests about the middle of the ground-bait.

Then take a second rod, and cast in about a yard above, and your third a yard below the first rod; and stay the rods in the ground: but go yourself so far from the water-side, that you perceive nothing but the top of the floats, which you must watch most diligently. Then when you have a bite, you shall perceive the top of your float to sink suddenly into the water: yet, nevertheless, be not too hasty to run to your rods, until you see that the line goes clear away; then creep to the water-side, and give as much line as possibly you can: if it be a good Carp or Bream, they will go to the farther side of the river: then strike gently, and hold your rod at a bent, a little while; but if you both pull together, you are sure to lose your game, for either your line, or hook, or hold, will break: and after you have overcome them, they will make noble sport, and are very shy to be landed. The Carp is far stronger and more mettlesome than the Bream.

Much more is to be observed in this kind of fish and fishing, but it is far fitter for experience and discourse than paper. Only, thus much is necessary for you to know, and to be mindful and careful of, that if the Pike or Perch do breed in that river, they will be sure to bite first, and must first be taken. And for the most part they are very large; and will repair to your ground-bait, not that they will eat of it, but will feed and sport themselves among the young fry that gather about and hover over the bait.

The way to discern the Pike and to take him, if you mistrust your Bream hook, for I have taken a Pike a yard long several times at my Bream hooks, and sometimes he hath had the luck to share my line, may be thus:

Take a small Bleak, or Roach, or Gudgeon, and bait it; and set it, alive, among your rods, two feet deep from the cork, with a little red worm on the point of the hook: then take a few crumbs of white bread, or some of the ground-bait, and sprinkle it gently amongst your rods. If Mr. Pike be there, then the little fish will skip out of the water at his appearance, but the live-set bait is sure to be taken.

Thus continue your sport from four in the morning till eight, and if it be a gloomy windy day, they will bite all day long: but this is too long to stand to your rods, at one place; and it will spoil your evening sport that day, which is this.

About four of the clock in the afternoon repair to your baited place; and as soon as you come to the water-side, cast in one-half of the rest of your ground-bait, and stand off; then whilst the fish are gathering together, for there they will most certainly come for their supper, you may take a pipe of tobacco: and then, in with your three rods, as in the morning. You will find excellent sport that evening, till eight of the clock: then cast in the residue of your ground-bait, and next morning, by four of the clock, visit them again for four hours, which is the best sport of all; and after that, let them rest till you and your friends have a mind to more sport.

From St. James's-tide until Bartholomew-tide is the best; when they have had all the summer's food, they are the fattest.

Observe, lastly, that after three or four days' fishing together, your game will be very shy and wary, and you shall hardly get above a bite or two at a baiting: then your only way is to desist from your sport, about two or three days: and in the meantime, on the place you late baited, and again intend to bait, you shall take a turf of green but short grass, as big or bigger than a round trencher; to the top of this turf, on the green side, you shall, with a needle and green thread, fasten one by one, as many little red worms as will near cover all the turf: then take a round board or trencher, make a hole in the middle thereof, and through the turf placed on the board or trencher, with a string or cord as long as is fitting, tied to a pole, let it down to the bottom of the water, for the fish to feed upon without disturbance about two or three days; and after that you have drawn it away, you may fall to, and enjoy your former recreation.

B. A.

# THE FOURTH DAY—*continued*

## *On the Tench*

### CHAPTER XI

PISCATOR

THE Tench, the physician of fishes, is observed to love ponds better than rivers, and to love pits better than either: yet Camden observes, there is a river in Dorsetshire that abounds with Tenches, but doubtless they retire to the most deep and quiet places in it.

This fish hath very large fins, very small and smooth scales, a red circle about his eyes, which are big and of a gold colour, and from either angle of his mouth there hangs down a little barb. In every Tench's head there are two little stones which foreign physicians make great use of, but he is not commended for wholesome meat, though there be very much use made of them for outward applications. Rondeletius says, that at his being at Rome, he saw a great cure done by applying a Tench to the feet of a very sick man. This, he says, was done after an unusual manner, by certain Jews. And it is observed that many of those people have many secrets yet unknown to Christians; secrets that have never yet been written, but have been since the days of their Solomon, who knew the nature of all things, even from the cedar to the shrub, delivered by tradition, from the father to the son, and so from generation to generation, without writing; or, unless it were casually, without the least communicating them to any other nation or tribe; for to do that they account a profanation. And, yet, it is thought that they, or some spirit worse than they, first told us, that lice, swallowed alive, were a certain cure for the yellow-jaundice. This, and many other medicines, were discovered by them, or by revelation; for, doubtless, we attained them not by study.

Well, this fish, besides his eating, is very useful, both dead and alive, for the good of mankind. But I will meddle no more with that, my honest, humble art teaches no such boldness: there are too many foolish meddlers in physick and divinity that think themselves fit to meddle with hidden secrets, and so bring destruction to their followers. But I'll not meddle with them, any farther than to wish them wiser; and shall tell you next, for I hope I may be so bold, that the Tench is the physician of fishes, for the Pike especially, and that the Pike, being either sick or hurt, is cured by the touch of the Tench. And it is observed that the tyrant Pike will not be a wolf to his physician, but forbears to devour him though he be never so hungry.

This fish, that carries a natural balsam in him to cure both himself and others, loves yet to feed in very foul water, and amongst weeds. And yet, I am sure, he eats pleasantly, and, doubtless, you will think so too, if you taste him. And I shall therefore proceed to give you some few, and but a few, directions how to catch this Tench, of which I have given you these observations.

He will bite at a paste made of brown bread and honey, or at a Marsh-worm, or a lob-worm; he inclines very much to any paste with which tar is mixt, and he will bite also at a smaller worm with his head nipped off, and a cod-worm put on the hook before that worm. And I doubt not but that he will also, in the three hot months, for in the nine colder he stirs not much, bite at a flag-worm or at a green gentle; but can positively say no more of the Tench, he being a fish I have not often angled for; but I wish my honest scholar may, and be ever fortunate when he fishes.

# THE FOURTH DAY—*continued*

## *On the Perch*

## CHAPTER XII

### PISCATOR AND VENATOR

PISCATOR. The Perch is a very good and very bold biting fish. He is one of the fishes of prey that, like the Pike and Trout, carries his teeth in his mouth, which is very large: and he dare venture to kill and devour several other kinds of fish. He has a hooked or hog back, which is armed with sharp and stiff bristles, and all his skin armed, or covered over with thick dry hard scales, and hath, which few other fish have, two fins on his back. He is so bold that he will invade one of his own kind, which the Pike will not do so willingly; and you may, therefore, easily believe him to be a bold biter.

The Perch is of great esteem in Italy, saith Aldrovandus: and especially the least are there esteemed a dainty dish. And Gesner prefers the Perch and Pike above the Trout, or any fresh-water fish: he says the Germans have this proverb, "More wholesome than a Perch of Rhine": and he says the River-Perch is so wholesome, that physicians allow him to be eaten by wounded men, or by men in fevers, or by women in child-bed.

He spawns but once a year; and is, by physicians, held very nutritive; yet, by many, to be hard of digestion. They abound more in the river Po, and in England, says Rondeletius, than other parts: and have in their brain a stone, which is, in foreign parts, sold by apothecaries, being there noted to be very medicinable against the stone in the reins. These be a part of the commendations which some philosophical brains have bestowed upon the freshwater Perch: yet they commend the Sea-Perch which is known by having but one fin on his back, of which they say we English see but a few, to be a much better fish.

The Perch grows slowly, yet will grow, as I have been credibly informed, to be almost two feet long; for an honest informer told me, such a one was not long since taken by Sir Abraham Williams, a gentleman of worth, and a brother of the angle, that yet lives, and I wish he may: this was a deep-bodied fish, and doubtless durst have devoured a Pike of half his own length. For I have told you, he is a bold fish; such a one as but for extreme hunger the Pike will not devour. For to affright the Pike, and save himself, the Perch will set up his fins, much like as a turkey-cock will sometimes set up his tail.

But, my scholar, the Perch is not only valiant to defend himself, but he is, as I said, a bold-biting fish: yet he will not bite at all seasons of the year; he is very abstemious in winter, yet will bite then in the midst of the day, if it be warm: and note, that all fish bite best about the midst of a warm day in winter. And he hath been observed, by some, not usually to bite till the mulberry-tree buds; that is to say, till extreme frosts be past the spring; for, when the mulberry-tree blossoms, many gardeners observe their forward fruit to be past the danger of frosts; and some have made the like observation of the Perch's biting.

But bite the Perch will, and that very boldly. And, as one has wittily observed, if there be twenty or forty in a hole, they may be, at one standing, all catched one after another; they being, as he says, like the wicked of the world, not afraid, though their fellows and companions perish in their sight. And you may observe, that they are not like the solitary Pike, but love to accompany one another, and march together in troops.

And the baits for this bold fish are not many: I mean, he will bite as well at some, or at any of these three, as at any or all others whatsoever: a worm, a minnow, or a little frog, of which you may find many in hay-time. And of worms; the dung-hill worm called a brandling I take to be best, being well scoured in moss or fennel; or he will bite at a worm that lies under cow-dung, with a bluish head. And if you rove for a Perch with a minnow, then it is best to be alive; you sticking your hook through his back fin; or a minnow with the hook in his upper lip, and letting him swim up and down, about mid-water, or a little lower, and you still keeping him to about that depth by a cork, which ought not to be a very little one: and the like way you are to fish for the Perch with a small frog, your hook being fastened through the skin of his leg, towards the upper part of it: and, lastly, I will give you but this advice, that you give the Perch time enough when he bites; for there was scarce ever any angler that has given him too much. And now I think best to rest myself; for I have almost spent my spirits with talking so long.

VENATOR. Nay, good master, one fish more, for you see it rains still: and you know our angles are like money put to usury; they may thrive, though we sit still, and do nothing but talk and enjoy one another. Come, come, the other fish, good master.

PISCATOR. But, scholar, have you nothing to mix with this discourse, which now grows both tedious and tiresome? Shall I have nothing from you, that seem to have both a good memory and a cheerful spirit?

VENATOR. Yes, master, I will speak you a copy of verses that were made by Doctor Donne, and made to shew the world that he could make soft and smooth verses, when he thought smoothness worth his labour: and I love them the better, because they allude to Rivers, and Fish and Fishing. They be these:

Come, live with me, and be my love,
And we will some new pleasures prove,
Of golden sands, and crystal brooks,
With silken lines, and silver hooks.

There will the river whisp'ring run,
Warm'd by thy eyes more than the sun;
And there the enamel'd fish will stay,
Begging themselves they may betray.

When thou wilt swim in that live bath,
Each fish, which every channel hath,
Most amorously to thee will swim,
Gladder to catch thee, than thou him.

If thou, to be so seen, beest loath
By sun or moon, thou dark'nest both;
And if mine eyes have leave to see,
I need not their light, having thee.

Let others freeze with angling reeds,
And cut their legs with shells and weeds,
Or treacherously poor fish beset
With strangling snares or windowy net;

Let coarse bold hands, from slimy nest,
The bedded fish in banks outwrest;
Let curious traitors sleave silk flies,
To 'witch poor wand'ring fishes' eyes.

For thee, thou need'st no such deceit,
For thou thyself art thine own bait;
That fish that is not catcht thereby,
Is wiser afar, alas, than I.

PISCATOR. Well remembered, honest scholar. I thank you for these choice verses; which I have heard formerly, but had quite forgot, till they were recovered by your happy memory. Well, being I have now rested myself a little, I will make you some requital, by telling you some observations of the Eel; for it rains still: and because, as you say, our angles are as money put to use, that thrives when we play, therefore we'll sit still, and enjoy ourselves a little longer under this honeysuckle hedge.

# THE FOURTH DAY—*continued*

## *Of the Eel, and other Fish that want Scales*

### CHAPTER XIII

PISCATOR

IT is agreed by most men, that the Eel is a most dainty fish: the Romans have esteemed her the Helena of their feasts; and some the queen of palate-pleasure. But most men differ about their breeding: some say they breed by generation, as other fish do; and others, that they breed, as some worms do, of mud; as rats and mice, and many other living creatures, are bred in Egypt, by the sun's heat when it shines upon the overflowing of the river Nilus; or out of the putrefaction of the earth, and divers other ways. Those that deny them to breed by generation, as other fish do, ask, If any man ever saw an Eel to have a spawn or melt? And they are answered, That they may be as certain of their breeding as if they had seen spawn; for they say, that they are certain that Eels have all parts fit for generation, like other fish, but so small as not to be easily discerned, by reason of their fatness; but that discerned they may be; and that the He and the She Eel may be distinguished by their fins. And Rondeletius says, he has seen Eels cling together like dew-worms.

And others say, that Eels, growing old, breed other Eels out of the corruption of their own age; which, Sir Francis Bacon says, exceeds not ten years. And others say, that as pearls are made of glutinous dewdrops, which are condensed by the sun's heat in those countries, so Eels are bred of a particular dew, falling in the months of May or June on the banks of some particular ponds or rivers, apted by nature for that end; which in a few days are, by the sun's heat, turned into Eels: and some of the Ancients have called the Eels that are thus bred, the offspring of Jove. I have seen, in the beginning of July, in a river not far from Canterbury, some parts of it covered over with young Eels, about the thickness of a straw; and these Eels did lie on the top of that water, as thick as motes are said to be in the sun: and I have heard the like of other rivers, as namely, in Severn, where they are called Yelvers; and in a pond, or mere near unto Staffordshire, where, about a set time in summer, such small Eels abound so much, that many of the poorer sort of people that inhabit near to it, take such Eels out of this mere with sieves or sheets; and make a kind of Eel-cake of them, and eat it like as bread. And Gesner quotes Venerable Bede, to say, that in England there is an island called Ely, by reason of the innumerable number of Eels that breed in it. But that Eels may be bred as some worms, and some kind of bees and wasps are, either of dew, or out of the corruption of the earth, seems to be made probable by the barnacles and young goslings bred by the sun's heat and the rotten planks of an old ship, and hatched of trees; both which are related for truths by Du Bartas and Lobel, and also by our learned Camden, and laborious Gerhard in his *Herbal*.

It is said by Rondeletius, that those Eels that are bred in rivers that relate to or be nearer to the sea, never return to the fresh waters, as the Salmon does always desire to do, when they have once tasted the salt water; and I do the more easily believe this, because I am certain that powdered beef is a most excellent bait to catch an Eel. And though Sir Francis Bacon will allow the Eel's life to be but ten years, yet he, in his *History of Life and Death*, mentions a Lamprey, belonging to the Roman emperor, to be made tame, and so kept for almost threescore years; and that such useful and pleasant observations were made of this Lamprey, that Crassus the orator, who kept her, lamented her death; and we read in Doctor Hakewill, that Hortensius was seen to weep at the death of a Lamprey that he had kept long, and loved exceedingly.

It is granted by all, or most men, that Eels, for about six months, that is to say, the six cold months of the year, stir not up or down, neither in the rivers, nor in the pools in which they usually are, but get into the soft earth or mud; and there many of them together bed themselves, and live without feeding upon anything, as I have told you some swallows have been observed to do in hollow trees, for those six cold months. And this the Eel and Swallow do, as not being able to endure winter weather: for Gesner quotes Albertus to say, that in the year 1125, that year's winter being more cold than usually, Eels did, by nature's instinct, get out of the water into a stack of hay in a meadow upon dry ground; and there bedded themselves: but yet, at last, a frost killed them. And our Camden relates, that, in Lancashire, fishes were digged out of the earth with spades, where no water was near to the place. I shall say little more of the Eel, but that, as it is observed he is impatient of cold, so it hath been observed, that, in warm weather, an Eel has been known to live five days out of the water.

And lastly, let me tell you, that some curious searchers into the natures of fish observe, that there be several sorts or kinds of Eels; as the silver Eel, the green or greenish Eel, with which the river of Thames abounds, and those are called Grigs; and a blackish Eel, whose head is more flat and bigger than ordinary Eels; and also an Eel whose fins are reddish, and but seldom taken in this nation, and yet taken sometimes. These several kind of Eels are, say some, diversely bred; as, namely, out of the corruption of the earth; and some by dew, and other ways, as I have said to you: and yet it is affirmed by some for a certain, that the silver Eel is bred by generation, but not by spawning as other fish do; but that her brood come alive from her, being then little live Eels no bigger nor longer than a pin; and I have had too many testimonies of this, to doubt the truth of it myself; and if I thought it needful I might prove it, but I think it is needless.

And this Eel, of which I have said so much to you, may be caught with divers kinds of baits: as namely, with powdered beef; with a lob or garden worm; with a minnow; or gut of a hen, chicken, or the guts of any fish, or with almost anything, for he is a greedy fish. But the Eel may be caught, especially, with a little, a very little Lamprey, which some call a Pride, and may, in the hot months, be found many of them in the river Thames, and in many mud-heaps in other rivers; yea, almost as usually as one finds worms in a dunghill.

Next note, that the Eel seldom stirs in the day, but then hides himself; and therefore he is usually caught by night, with one of these baits of which I have spoken; and may be then caught by laying hooks, which you are to fasten to the bank, or twigs of a tree; or by throwing a string across the stream, with many hooks at it, and those baited with the aforesaid baits; and a clod, or plummet, or stone, thrown into the river with this line, that so you may in the morning find it near to some fixed place; and then take it up with a drag-hook, or otherwise. But these things are, indeed, too common to be spoken of; and an hour's fishing with any angler will teach you better, both for these and many other common things in the practical part of angling, than a week's discourse. I shall therefore conclude this direction for taking the Eel, by telling you, that in a warm day in summer, I have taken many a good Eel by Snigling, and have been much pleased with that sport.

And because you, that are but a young angler, know not what Snigling is, I will now teach it to you. You remember I told you that Eels do not usually stir in the daytime; for then they hide themselves under some covert; or under boards or planks about flood-gates, or weirs, or mills: or in holes on the river banks: so that you, observing your time in a warm day, when the water is lowest, may take a strong small hook, tied to a strong line, or to a string about a yard long; and then into one of these holes, or between any boards about a mill, or under any great stone or plank, or any place where you think an Eel may hide or shelter herself, you may, with the help of a short stick, put in your bait, but leisurely, and as far as you may conveniently; and it is scarce to be doubted, but if there be an Eel within the sight of it, the Eel will bite instantly, and as certainly gorge it; and you need not doubt to have him if you pull him not out of the hole too quickly, but pull him out by degrees; for he, lying folded double in his hole, will, with the help of his tail, break all, unless you give him time to be wearied with pulling, and so get him out by degrees, not pulling too hard.

And to commute for your patient hearing this long direction, I shall next tell you, How to make this Eel a most excellent dish of meat.

First, wash him in water and salt; then pull off his skin below his vent or navel, and not much further: having done that, take out his guts as clean as you can, but wash him not: then give him three or four scotches with a knife; and then put into his belly and those scotches, sweet herbs, an anchovy, and a little nutmeg grated or cut very small, and your herbs and anchovies must also be cut very small; and mixt with good butter and salt: having done this, then pull his skin over him, all but his head, which you are to cut off, to the end you may tie his skin about that part where his head grew, and it must be so tied as to keep all his moisture within his skin: and having done this, tie him with tape or packthread to a spit, and roast him leisurely; and baste him with water and salt till his skin breaks, and then with butter; and having roasted him enough, let what was put into his belly, and what he drips, be his sauce. S. F.

When I go to dress an Eel thus, I wish he were as long and as big as that which was caught in Peterborough river, in the year 1667; which was a yard and three quarters long. If you will not believe me, then go and see at one of the coffee-houses in King Street in Westminster.

But now let me tell you, that though the Eel, thus drest, be not only excellent good, but more harmless than any other way, yet it is certain that physicians account the Eel dangerous meat; I will advise you therefore, as Solomon says of honey, "Hast thou found it, eat no more than is sufficient, lest thou surfeit, for it is not good to eat much honey." And let me add this, that the uncharitable Italian bids us "give Eels and no wine to our enemies."

And I will beg a little more of your attention, to tell you, that Aldrovandus, and divers physicians, commend the Eel very much for medicine, though not for meat. But let me tell you one observation, that the Eel is never out of season; as Trouts, and most other fish, are at set times; at least, most Eels are not.

I might here speak of many other fish, whose shape and nature are much like the Eel, and frequent both the sea and fresh rivers; as, namely, the Lamprel, the Lamprey, and the Lamperne: as also of the mighty Conger, taken often in Severn, about Gloucester: and might also tell in what high esteem many of them are for the curiosity of their taste. But these are not so proper to be talked of by me, because they make us anglers no sport; therefore I will let them alone, as the Jews do, to whom they are forbidden by their law.

And, scholar, there is also a FLOUNDER, a sea-fish which will wander very far into fresh rivers, and there lose himself and dwell: and thrive to a hand's breadth, and almost twice so long: a fish without scales, and most excellent meat: and a fish that affords much sport to the angler, with any small worm, but especially a little bluish worm, gotten out of marsh-ground, or meadows, which should be well scoured. But this, though it be most excellent meat, yet it wants scales, and is, as I told you, therefore an abomination to the Jews.

But, scholar, there is a fish that they in Lancashire boast very much of, called a CHAR; taken there, and I think there only, in a mere called Winander Mere; a mere, says Camden, that is the largest in this nation, being ten miles in length, and some say as smooth in the bottom as if it were paved with polished marble. This fish never exceeds fifteen or sixteen inches in length; and is spotted like a Trout: and has scarce a bone, but on the back. But this, though I do not know whether it make the angler sport, yet I would have you take notice of it, because it is a rarity, and of so high esteem with persons of great note.

Nor would I have you ignorant of a rare fish called a GUINIAD; of which I shall tell you what Camden and others speak. The river Dee, which runs by Chester, springs in Merionethshire; and, as it runs toward Chester, it runs through Pemble Mere, which is a large water: and it is observed, that though the river Dee abounds with Salmon, and Pemble mere with the Guiniad, yet there is never any Salmon caught in the mere, nor a Guiniad in the river. And now my next observation shall be of the Barbel.

# THE FOURTH DAY—*continued*

## *Of the Barbel*

### CHAPTER XIV

PISCATOR, VENATOR, MILK-WOMAN

PISCATOR. The Barbel is so called, says Gesner, by reason of his barb or wattles at his mouth, which are under his nose or chaps. He is one of those leather-mouthed fishes that I told you of, that does very seldom break his hold if he be once hooked: but he is so strong, that he will often break both rod and line, if he proves to be a big one.

But the Barbel, though he be of a fine shape, and looks big, yet he is not accounted the best fish to eat, neither for his wholesomeness nor his taste; but the male is reputed much better than the female, whose spawn is very hurtful, as I will presently declare to you.

They flock together like sheep, and are at the worst in April, about which time they spawn; but quickly grow to be in season. He is able to live in the strongest swifts of the water: and, in summer, they love the shallowest and sharpest streams: and love to lurk under weeds, and to feed on gravel, against a rising ground; and will root and dig in the sands with his nose like a hog, and there nests himself: yet sometimes he retires to deep and swift bridges, or flood-gates, or weir; where he will nest himself amongst piles, or in hollow places; and take such hold of moss or weeds, that be the water never so swift, it is not able to force him from the place that he contends for. This is his constant custom in summer, when he and most living creatures sport themselves in the sun: but at the approach of winter, then he forsakes the swift streams and shallow waters, and, by degrees, retires to those parts of the river that are quiet and deeper; in which places, and I think about that time he spawns; and, as I have formerly told you, with the help of the melter, hides his spawn or eggs in holes, which they both dig in the gravel; and then they mutually labour to cover it with the same sand, to prevent it from being devoured by other fish.

There be such store of this fish in the river Danube, that Rondeletius says they may, in some places of it, and in some months of the year, be taken, by those who dwell near to the river, with their hands, eight or ten load at a time. He says, they begin to be good in May, and that they cease to be so in August: but it is found to be otherwise in this nation. But thus far we agree with him, that the spawn of a Barbel, if it be not poison, as he says, yet that it is dangerous meat, and especially in the month of May, which is so certain, that Gesner and Gasius declare it had an ill effect upon them, even to the endangering of their lives.

The fish is of a fine cast and handsome shape, with small scales, which are placed after a most exact and curious manner, and, as I told you, may be rather said not to be ill, than to be good meat. The Chub and he have, I think, both lost part of their credit by ill cookery; they being reputed the worst, or coarsest, of fresh-water fish. But the Barbel affords an angler choice sport, being a lusty and a cunning fish; so lusty and cunning as to endanger the breaking of the angler's line, by running his head forcibly towards any covert, or hole, or bank, and then striking at the line, to break it off, with his tail; as is observed by Plutarch, in his book *De Industriâ Animalium:* and also so cunning, to nibble and suck off your worm close to the hook, and yet avoid the letting the hook come into his mouth.

The Barbel is also curious for his baits; that is to say, that they be clean and sweet; that is to say, to have your worms well scoured, and not kept in sour and musty moss, for he is a curious feeder: but at a well-scoured lob-worm he will bite as boldly as at any bait, and specially if, the night or two before you fish for him, you shall bait the places where you intend to fish for him, with big worms cut into pieces. And note, that none did ever over-bait the place, nor fish too early or too late for a Barbel. And the Barbel will bite also at gentles, which, not being too much scoured, but green, are a choice bait for him: and so is cheese, which is not to be too hard, but kept a day or two in a wet linen cloth, to make it tough; with this you may also bait the water a day or two before you fish for the Barbel, and be much the likelier to catch store; and if the cheese were laid in clarified honey a short time before, as namely, an hour or two, you were still the likelier to catch fish. Some have directed to cut the cheese into thin pieces, and toast it; and then tie it on the hook with fine silk. And some advise to fish for the Barbel with sheep's tallow and soft cheese, beaten or worked into a paste; and that it is choicely good in August: and I believe it. But, doubtless, the lob-worm well scoured, and the gentle not too much scoured, and cheese ordered as I have directed, are baits enough, and I think will serve in any month: though I shall commend any angler that tries conclusions, and is industrious to improve the art. And now, my honest scholar, the long shower and my tedious discourse are both ended together: and I shall give you but this observation, that when you fish for a Barbel, your rod and line be both long and of good strength; for, as I told you, you will find him a heavy and a dogged fish to be dealt withal; yet he seldom or never breaks his hold, if he be once strucken. And if you would know more of fishing for the Umber or Barbel, get into favour with Dr. Sheldon, whose skill is above others; and of that, the poor that dwell about him have a comfortable experience.

And now let's go and see what interest the Trouts will pay us, for letting our angle-rods lie so long and so quietly in the water for their use. Come, scholar, which will you take up?

VENATOR. Which you think fit, master.

PISCATOR. Why, you shall take up that; for I am certain, by viewing the line, it has a fish at it. Look you, scholar! well done! Come, now take up the other too: well! now you may tell my brother Peter, at night, that you have caught a leash of Trouts this day. And now let's move towards our lodging, and drink a draught of red-cow's milk as we go; and give pretty Maudlin and her honest mother a brace of Trouts for their supper.

VENATOR. Master, I like your motion very well: and I think it is now about milking-time; and yonder they be at it.

PISCATOR. God speed you, good woman! I thank you both for our songs last night: I and my companion have had such fortune a-fishing this day, that we resolve to give you and Maudlin a brace of Trouts for supper; and we will now taste a draught of your red-cow's milk.

MILK-WOMAN. Marry, and that you shall with all my heart; and I will be still your debtor when you come this way. If you will but speak the word, I will make you a good syllabub of new verjuice; and then you may sit down in a haycock, and eat it; and Maudlin shall sit by and sing you the good old song of the "Hunting in Chevy Chace," or some other good ballad, for she hath store of them: Maudlin, my honest Maudlin, hath a notable memory, and she thinks nothing too good for you, because you be such honest men.

VENATOR. We thank you; and intend, once in a month to call upon you again, and give you a little warning; and so, good-night. Good-night, Maudlin. And now, good master, let's lose no time: but tell me somewhat more of fishing; and if you please, first, something of fishing for a Gudgeon.

PISCATOR. I will, honest scholar.

## THE FOURTH DAY—*continued*

### *Of the Gudgeon, the Ruffe, and the Bleak*

### CHAPTER XV

PISCATOR

THE Gudgeon is reputed a fish of excellent taste, and to be very wholesome. He is of a fine shape, of a silver colour, and beautified with black spots both on his body and tail. He breeds two or three times in the year; and always in summer. He is commended for a fish of excellent nourishment. The Germans call him Groundling, by reason of his feeding on the ground; and he there feasts himself, in sharp streams and on the gravel. He and the Barbel both feed so: and do not hunt for flies at any time, as most other fishes do. He is an excellent fish to enter a young angler, being easy to be taken with a small red worm, on or very near to the ground. He is one of those leather-mouthed fish that has his teeth in his throat, and will hardly be lost off from the hook if he be once strucken.

They be usually scattered up and down every river in the shallows, in the heat of summer: but in autumn, when the weeds begin to grow sour and rot, and the weather colder, then they gather together, and get into the deeper parts of the water; and are to be fished for there, with your hook always touching the ground, if you fish for him with a float or with a cork. But many will fish for the Gudgeon by hand, with a running line upon the ground, without a cork, as a Trout is fished for: and it is an excellent way, if you have a gentle rod, and as gentle a hand.

There is also another fish called a POPE, and by some a RUFFE; a fish that is not known to be in some rivers: he is much like the Perch for his shape, and taken to be better than the Perch, but will not grow to be bigger than a Gudgeon. He is an excellent fish; no fish that swims is of a pleasanter taste. And he is also excellent to enter a young angler, for he is a greedy biter: and they will usually lie, abundance of them together, in one reserved place, where the water is deep and runs quietly; and an easy angler, if he has found where they lie, may catch forty or fifty, or sometimes twice so many, at a standing.

You must fish for him with a small red worm; and if you bait the ground with earth, it is excellent.

There is also a BLEAK or fresh-water Sprat; a fish that is ever in motion, and therefore called by some the river-swallow; for just as you shall observe the swallow to be, most evenings in summer, ever in motion, making short and quick turns when he flies to catch flies, in the air, by which he lives; so does the Bleak at the top of the water. Ausonius would have called him Bleak from his whitish colour: his back is of a pleasant sad or sea-water-green; his belly, white and shining as the mountain snow. And doubtless, though we have the fortune, which virtue has in poor people, to be neglected, yet the Bleak ought to be much valued, though we want Allamot salt, and the skill that the Italians have, to turn them into anchovies. This fish may be caught with a Pater-noster line; that is, six or eight very small hooks tied along the line, one half a foot above the other: I have seen five caught thus at one time; and the bait has been gentles, than which none is better.

Or this fish may be caught with a fine small artificial fly, which is to be of a very sad brown colour, and very small, and the hook answerable. There is no better sport than whipping for Bleaks in a boat, or on a bank, in the swift water, in a summer's evening, with a hazel top about five or six foot long, and a line twice the length of the rod. I have heard Sir Henry Wotton say, that there be many that in Italy will catch swallows so, or especially martins; this bird-angler standing on the top of a steeple to do it, and with the line twice so long as I have spoken of. And let me tell you, scholar, that both Martins and Bleaks be most excellent meat.

And let me tell you, that I have known a Heron, that did constantly frequent one place, caught with a hook baited with a big minnow or a small gudgeon. The line and hook must be strong: and tied to some loose staff, so big as she cannot fly away with it: a line not exceeding two yards.

# THE FOURTH DAY—*continued*

*Is of nothing, or of nothing worth*

## CHAPTER XVI

PISCATOR, VENATOR, PETER, CORIDON

PISCATOR. My purpose was to give you some directions concerning ROACH and DACE, and some other inferior fish which make the angler excellent sport; for you know there is more pleasure in hunting the hare than in eating her: but I will forbear, at this time, to say any more, because you see yonder come our brother Peter and honest Coridon. But I will promise you, that as you and I fish and walk to-morrow towards London, if I have now forgotten anything that I can then remember, I will not keep it from you.

Well met, gentlemen; this is lucky that we meet so just together at this very door, Come, hostess, where are you? is supper ready? Come, first give us a drink; and be as quick as you can, for I believe we are all very hungry. Well, brother Peter and Coridon, to you both! Come, drink: and then tell me what luck of fish: we two have caught but ten trouts, of which my scholar caught three. Look! here's eight; and a brace we gave away. We have had a most pleasant day for fishing and talking, and are returned home both weary and hungry; and now meat and rest will be pleasant.

PETER. And Coridon and I have not had an unpleasant day: and yet I have caught but five trouts; for, indeed, we went to a good honest alehouse, and there we played at shovel-board half the day; all the time that it rained we were there, and as merry as they that fished. And I am glad we are now with a dry house over our heads; for, hark! how it rains and blows. Come, hostess, give us more ale, and our supper with what haste you may: and when we have supped, let us have your song, Piscator; and the catch that your scholar promised us; or else, Coridon will be dogged.

PISCATOR. Nay, I will not be worse than my word; you shall not want my song, and I hope I shall be perfect in it.

VENATOR. And I hope the like for my catch, which I have ready too: and therefore let's go merrily to supper, and then have a gentle touch at singing and drinking; but the last with moderation.

CORIDON. Come, now for your song; for we have fed heartily. Come, hostess, lay a few more sticks on the fire. And now, sing when you will.

PISCATOR. Well then, here's to you, Coridon; and now for my song.

O the gallant Fisher's life,
It is the best of any;
'Tis full of pleasure, void of strife,
And 'tis beloved of many:
Other joys
Are but toys;
Only this
Lawful is;
For our skill
Breeds no ill,
But content and pleasure.

In a morning up we rise,
Ere Aurora's peeping;
Drink a cup to wash our eyes;
Leave the sluggard sleeping;
Then we go
To and fro,
With our knacks
At our backs,
To such streams
As the Thames,
If we have the leisure.

When we please to walk abroad
For our recreation,
In the fields is our abode,
Full of delectation:
Where in a brook
With a hook,
Or a lake,
Fish we take:
There we sit,
For a bit,
Till we fish entangle.

We have gentles in a horn,
We have paste and worms too;
We can watch both night and morn,
Suffer rain and storms too;
None do here

Use to swear;
Oaths do fray
Fish away;
We sit still,
And watch our quill;
Fishers must not wrangle.

If the sun's excessive heat
Make our bodies swelter,
To an osier hedge we get
For a friendly shelter;
Where, in a dike,
Perch or Pike,
Roach or Dace,
We do chase;
Bleak or Gudgeon,
Without grudging:
We are still contented.

Or we sometimes pass an hour
Under a green willow,
That defends us from a shower,
Making earth our pillow;
Where we may
Think and pray
Before death
Stops our breath.
Other joys
Are but toys,
And to be lamented.

JO. CHALKHILL.

VENATOR. Well sung, master; this day's fortune and pleasure, and the night's company and song, do all make me more and more in love with angling. Gentlemen, my master left me alone for an hour this day; and I verily believe he retired himself from talking with me that he might be so perfect in this song; was it not, master?

PISCATOR. Yes indeed, for it is many years since I learned it; and having forgotten a part of it, I was forced to patch it up with the help of mine own invention, who am not excellent at poetry, as my part of the song may testify; but of that I will say no more, lest you should think I mean, by discommending it, to beg your commendations of it. And therefore, without replications, let's hear your catch, scholar; which I hope will be a good one, for you are both musical and have a good fancy to boot.

VENATOR. Marry, and that you shall; and as freely as I would have my honest master tell me some more secrets of fish and fishing, as we walk and fish towards London to-morrow. But, master, first let me tell you, that very hour which you were absent from me, I sat down under a willow-tree by the water-side, and considered what you had told me of the owner of that pleasant meadow in which you then left me; that he had a plentiful estate, and not a heart to think so; that he had at this time many law-suits depending; and that they both damped his mirth, and took up so much of his time and thoughts, that he himself had not leisure to take the sweet content that I, who pretended no title to them, took in his fields: for I could there sit quietly; and looking on the water, see some fishes sport themselves in the silver streams, others leaping at flies of several shapes and colours; looking on the hills, I could behold them spotted with woods and groves; looking down the meadows, could see, here a boy gathering lilies and lady-smocks, and there a girl cropping culverkeys and cowslips, all to make garlands suitable to this present month of May: these, and many other field flowers, so perfumed the air, that I thought that very meadow like that field in Sicily of which Diodorus speaks, where the perfumes arising from the place make all dogs that hunt in it to fall off, and to lose their hottest scent. I say, as I thus sat, joying in my own happy condition, and pitying this poor rich man that owned this and many other pleasant groves and meadows about me, I did thankfully remember what my Saviour said, that the meek possess the earth; or rather, they enjoy what the others possess, and enjoy not; for anglers and meek quiet-spirited men are free from those high, those restless thoughts, which corrode the sweets of life; and they, and they only, can say, as the poet has happily exprest it,

Hail! blest estate of lowliness;
  Happy enjoyments of such minds
As, rich in self-contentedness,
  Can, like the reeds, in roughest winds,
By yielding make that blow but small
At which proud oaks and cedars fall.

There came also into my mind at that time, certain verses in praise of a mean estate and humble mind: they were written by Phineas Fletcher, an excellent divine, and an excellent angler; and the author of excellent *Piscatory Eclogues*, in which you shall see the picture of this good man's mind: and I wish mine to be like it.

No empty hopes, no courtly fears him fright;
No begging wants his middle fortune bite:
But sweet content exiles both misery and spite.

His certain life, that never can deceive him,
  Is full of thousand sweets, and rich content;
The smooth-leav'd beeches in the field receive him,

With coolest shade, till noon-tide's heat be spent.
His life is neither tost in boisterous seas,
Or the vexatious world, or lost in slothful ease;
Pleas'd and full blest he lives, when he his God can please.

His bed, more safe than soft, yields quiet sleeps,
While by his side his faithful spouse has place;
His little son into his bosom creeps,
The lively picture of his father's face.
His humble house or poor state ne'er torment him;
Less he could like, if less his God had lent him;
And when he dies, green turfs do for a tomb content him.

Gentlemen, these were a part of the thoughts that then possessed me. And I there made a conversion of a piece of an old catch, and added more to it, fitting them to be sung by us anglers. Come, Master, you can sing well: you must sing a part of it, as it is in this paper.

Man's life is but vain, for 'tis subject to pain,
And sorrow, and short as a bubble;
'Tis a hodge-podge of business, and money, and care,
And care, and money, and trouble.

But we'll take no care when the weather proves fair;
Nor will we vex now though it rain;
We'll banish all sorrow, and sing till to-morrow,
And angle, and angle again.

PETER. I marry, Sir, this is musick indeed; this has cheer'd my heart, and made me remember six verses in praise of musick, which I will speak to you instantly.

Musick! miraculous rhetorick, thou speak'st sense
Without a tongue, excelling eloquence;
With what ease might thy errors be excus'd,
Wert thou as truly lov'd as th' art abus'd!
But though dull souls neglect, and some reprove thee,
I cannot hate thee, 'cause the Angels love thee.

VENATOR. And the repetition of these last verses of musick has called to my memory what Mr. Edmund Waller, a lover of the angle, says of love and musick.

Whilst I listen to thy voice,
Chloris! I feel my heart decay;
That powerful voice
Calls my fleeting soul away:
Oh! suppress that magic sound,
Which destroys without a wound.

Peace, Chloris! peace, or singing die,
That together you and I
To heaven may go;
For all we know
Of what the blessed do above,
Is, that they sing, and that they love.

PISCATOR. Well remembered, brother Peter; these verses came seasonably, and we thank you heartily. Come, we will all join together, my host and all, and sing my scholar's catch over again; and then each man drink the tother cup, and to bed; and thank God we have a dry house over our heads.

PISCATOR. Well, now, good-night to everybody.

PETER. And so say I.

VENATOR. And so say I.

CORIDON. Good-night to you all; and I thank you.

## THE FIFTH DAY

PISCATOR. Good-morrow, brother Peter, and the like to you, honest Coridon.

Come, my hostess says there is seven shillings to pay: let's each man drink a pot for his morning's draught, and lay down his two shillings, so that my hostess may not have occasion to repent herself of being so diligent, and using us so kindly.

PETER. The motion is liked by everybody, and so, hostess, here's your money: we anglers are all beholden to you; it will not be long ere I'll see you again; and now, brother Piscator, I wish you, and my brother your scholar, a fair day and good fortune. Come, Coridon, this is our way.

# THE FIFTH DAY—*continued*

## *Of Roach and Dace*

### CHAPTER XVII

VENATOR AND PISCATOR

VENATOR. Good master, as we go now towards London, be still so courteous as to give me more instructions; for I have several boxes in my memory, in which I will keep them all very safe, there shall not one of them be lost.

PISCATOR. Well, scholar, that I will: and I will hide nothing from you that I can remember, and can think may help you forward towards a perfection in this art. And because we have so much time, and I have said so little of Roach and Dace, I will give you some directions concerning them.

Some say the Roach is so called from *rutilus*, which they say signifies red fins. He is a fish of no great reputation for his dainty taste; and his spawn is accounted much better than any other part of him. And you may take notice, that as the Carp is accounted the water-fox, for his cunning; so the Roach is accounted the water-sheep, for his simplicity or foolishness. It is noted, that the Roach and Dace recover strength, and grow in season in a fortnight after spawning; the Barbel and Chub in a month; the Trout in four months; and the Salmon in the like time, if he gets into the sea, and after into fresh water.

Roaches be accounted much better in the river than in a pond, though ponds usually breed the biggest. But there is a kind of bastard small Roach, that breeds in ponds, with a very forked tail, and of a very small size; which some say is bred by the Bream and right Roach; and some ponds are stored with these beyond belief; and knowing-men, that know their difference, call them Ruds: they differ from the true Roach, as much as a Herring from a Pilchard. And these bastard breed of Roach are now scattered in many rivers: but I think not in the Thames, which I believe affords the largest and fattest in this nation, especially below London Bridge. The Roach is a leather-mouthed fish, and has a kind of saw-like teeth in his throat. And lastly, let me tell you, the Roach makes an angler excellent sport, especially the great Roaches about London, where I think there be the best Roach-anglers. And I think the best Trout-anglers be in Derbyshire; for the waters there are clear to an extremity.

Next, let me tell you, you shall fish for this Roach in Winter, with paste or gentles; in April, with worms or cadis; in the very hot months, with little white snails; or with flies under water, for he seldom takes them at the top, though the Dace will. In many of the hot months, Roaches may also be caught thus: take a May-fly, or ant-fly, sink him with a little lead to the bottom, near to the piles or posts of a bridge, or near to any posts of a weir, I mean any deep place where Roaches lie quietly, and then pull your fly up very leisurely, and usually a Roach will follow your bait up to the very top of the water, and gaze on it there, and run at it, and take it, lest the fly should fly away from him.

I have seen this done at Windsor and Henley Bridge, and great store of Roach taken; and sometimes, a Dace or Chub. And in August you may fish for them with a paste made only of the crumbs of bread, which should be of pure fine manchet; and that paste must be so tempered betwixt your hands till it be both soft and tough too: a very little water, and time, and labour, and clean hands, will make it a most excellent paste. But when you fish with it, you must have a small hook, a quick eye, and a nimble hand, or the bait is lost, and the fish too; if one may lose that which he never had. With this paste you may, as I said, take both the Roach and the Dace or Dare; for they be much of a kind, in manner of feeding, cunning, goodness, and usually in size. And therefore take this general direction, for some other baits which may concern you to take notice of: they will bite almost at any fly, but especially at ant-flies; concerning which take this direction, for it is very good.

Take the blackish ant-fly out of the mole-hill or ant-hill, in which place you shall find them in the month of June; or if that be too early in the year, then, doubtless, you may find them in July, August, and most of September. Gather them alive, with both their wings: and then put them into a glass that will hold a quart or a pottle; but first put into the glass a handful, or more, of the moist earth out of which you gather them, and as much of the roots of the grass of the said hillock; and then put in the flies gently, that they lose not their wings: lay a clod of earth over it; and then so many as are put into the glass, without bruising, will live there a month or more, and be always in readiness for you to fish with: but if you would have them keep longer, then get any great earthen pot, or barrel of three or four gallons, which is better, then wash your barrel with water and honey; and having put into it a quantity of earth and grass roots, then put in your flies, and cover it, and they will live a quarter of a year. These, in any stream and clear water, are a deadly bait for Roach or Dace, or for a Chub: and your rule is to fish not less than a handful from the bottom.

I shall next tell you a winter-bait for a Roach, a Dace, or Chub; and it is choicely good. About All-hallantide, and so till frost comes, when you see men ploughing up heath ground, or sandy ground, or greenswards, then follow the plough, and you shall find a white worm, as big as two maggots, and it hath a red head: you may observe in what ground most are, for there the crows will be very watchful and follow the plough very close: it is all soft, and full of whitish guts; a worm that is, in Norfolk and some other counties, called a grub; and is bred of the spawn or eggs of a beetle, which she leaves in holes that she digs in the ground under cow or horse dung, and there rests all winter, and in March or April comes to be first a red and then a black beetle. Gather a thousand or two of these, and put them, with a peck or two of their own earth, into some tub or firkin, and cover and keep them so warm that the frost or cold air, or winds, kill them not: these you may keep all winter, and kill fish with them at any time; and if you put some of them into a little earth and honey, a day before you use them, you will find them an excellent bait for Bream, Carp, or indeed for almost any fish.

And after this manner you may also keep gentles all winter; which are a good bait then, and much the better for being lively and tough. Or you may breed and keep gentles thus: take a piece of beast's liver, and, with a cross stick, hang it in some corner, over a pot or barrel half full of dry clay; and as the gentles grow big, they will fall into the barrel and scour themselves, and be always ready for use whensoever you incline to fish; and these gentles may be thus created till after Michaelmas. But if you desire to keep gentles to fish with all the year, then get a dead cat, or a kite, and let it be fly-blown; and when the gentles begin to be alive and to stir, then bury it and them in soft moist earth, but as free from frost as you can; and these you may dig up at any time when you intend to use them: these will last till March, and about that time turn to be flies.

But if you be nice to foul your fingers, which good anglers seldom are, then take this bait: get a handful of well-made malt, and put it into a dish of water; and then wash and rub it betwixt your hands till you make it clean, and as free from husks as you can; then put that water from it, and put a small quantity of fresh water to it, and set it in something that is fit for that purpose, over the fire, where it is not to boil apace, but leisurely and very softly, until it become somewhat soft, which you may try by feeling it betwixt your finger and thumb; and when it is soft, then put your water from it: and then take a sharp knife, and turning the sprout end of the corn upward with the point of your knife, take the back part of the husk off from it, and yet leaving a kind of inward husk on the corn, or else it is marr'd; and then cut off that sprouted end, I mean a little of it, that the white may appear; and so pull off the husk on the cloven side, as I directed you; and then cutting off a very little of the other end, that so your hook may enter; and if your hook be small and good, you will find this to be a very choice bait, either for winter or summer, you sometimes casting a little of it into the place where your float swims.

And to take the Roach and Dace, a good bait is the young brood of wasps or bees, if you dip their heads in blood; especially good for Bream, if they be baked, or hardened in their husks in an oven, after the bread is taken out of it; or hardened on a fire-shovel: and so also is the thick blood of sheep, being half dried on a trencher, that so you may cut into such pieces as may best fit the size of your hook; and a little salt keeps it from growing black, and makes it not the worse, but better: this is taken to be a choice bait, if rightly ordered.

There be several oils of a strong smell that I have been told of, and to be excellent to tempt fish to bite, of which I could say much. But I remember I once carried a small bottle from Sir George Hastings to Sir Henry Wotton, they were both chemical men, as a great present: it was sent, and receiv'd, and us'd, with great confidence; and yet, upon inquiry, I found it did not answer the expectation of Sir Henry; which, with the help of this and other circumstances, makes me have little belief in such things as many men talk of. Not but that I think that fishes both smell and hear, as I have exprest in my former discourse: but there is a mysterious knack, which though it be much easier than the philosopher's stone, yet is not attainable by common capacities, or else lies locked up in the brain or breast of some chemical man, that, like the Rosicrucians, will not yet reveal it. But let me nevertheless tell you, that camphire, put with moss into your worm-bag with your worms, makes them, if many anglers be not very much mistaken, a tempting bait, and the angler more fortunate. But I stepped by chance into this discourse of oils, and fishes smelling; and though there might be more said, both of it and of baits for Roach and Dace and other float-fish, yet I will forbear it at this time, and tell you, in the next place, how you are to prepare your tackling: concerning which, I will, for sport sake, give you an old rhyme out of an old fish book; which will prove a part, and but a part, of what you are to provide.

My rod and my line, my float and my lead,
 My hook and my plummet, my whetstone and knife,
My basket, my baits, both living and dead,

My net, and my meat, for that is the chief:
Then I must have thread, and hairs green and small,
With mine angling purse: and so you have all.

But you must have all these tackling, and twice so many more, with which, if you mean to be a fisher, you must store yourself; and to that purpose I will go with you, either to Mr. Margrave, who dwells amongst the book-sellers in St. Paul's Church-yard, or to Mr. John Stubs, near to the Swan in Goldinglane: they be both honest men, and will fit an angler with what tackling he lacks.

VENATOR. Then, good master, let it be at —— for he is nearest to my dwelling. And I pray let's meet there the ninth of May next, about two of the clock; and I'll want nothing that a fisher should be furnished with.

PISCATOR. Well, and I'll not fail you, God willing, at the time and place appointed.

VENATOR. I thank you, good master, and I will not fail you. And, good master, tell me what BAITS more you remember; for it will not now be long ere we shall be at Tottenham-High-Cross; and when we come thither I will make you some requital of your pains, by repeating as choice a copy of Verses as any we have heard since we met together; and that is a proud word, for we have heard very good ones.

PISCATOR. Well, scholar, and I shall be then right glad to hear them. And I will, as we walk, tell you whatsoever comes in my mind, that I think may be worth your hearing. You may make another choice bait thus: take a handful or two of the best and biggest wheat you can get; boil it in a little milk, like as frumity is boiled; boil it so till it be soft; and then fry it, very leisurely, with honey, and a little beaten saffron dissolved in milk; and you will find this a choice bait, and good, I think, for any fish, especially for Roach, Dace, Chub, or Grayling: I know not but that it may be as good for a river Carp, and especially if the ground be a little baited with it.

And you may also note, that the SPAWN of most fish is a very tempting bait, being a little hardened on a warm tile and cut into fit pieces. Nay, mulberries, and those black-berries which grow upon briars, be good baits for Chubs or Carps: with these many have been taken in ponds, and in some rivers where such trees have grown near the water, and the fruit customarily dropt into it. And there be a hundred other baits, more than can be well named, which, by constant baiting the water, will become a tempting bait for any fish in it.

You are also to know, that there be divers kinds of CADIS, or Case-worms, that are to be found in this nation, in several distinct counties, in several little brooks that relate to bigger rivers; as namely, one cadis called a piper, whose husk, or case, is a piece of reed about an inch long, or longer, and as big about as the compass of a two-pence. These worms being kept three or four days in a woollen bag, with sand at the bottom of it, and the bag wet once a day, will in three or four days turn to be yellow; and these be a choice bait for the Chub or Chavender, or indeed for any great fish, for it is a large bait.

There is also a lesser cadis-worm, called a Cockspur, being in fashion like the spur of a cock, sharp at one end; and the case, or house, in which this dwells, is made of small husks, and gravel, and slime, most curiously made of these, even so as to be wondered at, but not to be made by man, no more than a king-fisher's nest can, which is made of little fishes' bones, and have such a geometrical interweaving and connection as the like is not to be done by the art of man. This kind of cadis is a choice bait for any float-fish; it is much less than the piper-cadis, and to be so ordered: and these may be so preserved, ten, fifteen, or twenty days, or it may be longer.

There is also another cadis, called by some a Straw-worm, and by some a Ruff-coat, whose house, or case, is made of little pieces of bents, and rushes, and straws, and water-weeds, and I know not what; which are so knit together with condensed slime, that they stick about her husk or case, not unlike the bristles of a hedge-hog. These three cadises are commonly taken in the beginning of summer; and are good, indeed, to take any kind of fish, with float or otherwise. I might tell you of many more, which as they do early, so those have their time also of turning to be flies in later summer; but I might lose myself, and tire you, by such a discourse: I shall therefore but remember you, that to know these, and their several kinds, and to what flies every particular cadis turns, and then how to use them, first as they be cadis, and after as they be flies, is an art, and an art that every one that professes to be an angler has not leisure to search after, and, if he had, is not capable of learning.

I'll tell you, scholar; several countries have several kinds of cadises, that indeed differ as much as dogs do; that is to say, as much as a very cur and a greyhound do. These be usually bred in the very little rills, or ditches, that run into bigger rivers; and I think a more proper bait for those very rivers than any other. I know not how, or of what, this cadis receives life, or what coloured fly it turns to; but doubtless they are the death of many Trouts: and this is one killing way:

Take one, or more if need be, of these large yellow cadis: pull off his head, and with it pull out his black gut; put the body, as little bruised as is possible, on a very little hook, armed on with a red hair, which will shew like the cadis-head; and a very little thin lead, so put upon the shank of the hook that it may sink presently. Throw this bait, thus ordered, which will look very yellow, into any great still hole where a Trout is, and he will presently venture his life for it, it is not to be doubted, if you be not espied; and that the bait first touch the water before the line. And this will do best in the deepest stillest water.

Next, let me tell you, I have been much pleased to walk quietly by a brook, with a little stick in my hand, with which I might easily take these, and consider the curiosity of their composure: and if you should ever like to do so, then note, that your stick must be a little hazel, or willow, cleft, or have a nick at one end of it, by which means you may, with ease, take many of them in that nick out of the water, before you have any occasion to use them. These, my honest scholar, are some observations, told to you as they now come suddenly into my memory, of which you may make some use: but for the practical part, it is that that makes an angler: it is diligence, and observation, and practice, and an ambition to be the best in the art, that must do it. I will tell you, scholar, I once heard one say, "I envy not him that eats better meat than I do; nor him that is richer, or that wears better clothes than I do: I envy nobody but him, and him only, that catches more fish than I do." And such a man is like to prove an angler; and this noble emulation I wish to you, and all young anglers.

# THE FIFTH DAY—*continued*

## *Of the Minnow, or Penk; Loach; Bull-Head, or Miller's-Thumb: and the Stickle-bag*

### CHAPTER XVIII

#### PISCATOR AND VENATOR

PISCATOR. There be also three or four other little fish that I had almost forgot; that are all without scales; and may for excellency of meat, be compared to any fish of greatest value and largest size. They be usually full of eggs or spawn, all the months of summer; for they breed often, as 'tis observed mice and many of the smaller four-footed creatures of the earth do; and as those, so these come quickly to their full growth and perfection. And it is needful that they breed both often and numerously; for they be, besides other accidents of ruin, both a prey and baits for other fish. And first I shall tell you of the Minnow or Penk.

The MINNOW hath, when he is in perfect season, and not sick, which is only presently after spawning, a kind of dappled or waved colour, like to a panther, on its sides, inclining to a greenish or sky-colour; his belly being milk white; and his back almost black or blackish. He is a sharp biter at a small worm, and in hot weather makes excellent sport for young anglers, or boys, or women that love that recreation. And in the spring they make of them excellent Minnow-tansies; for being washed well in salt, and their heads and tails cut off, and their guts taken out, and not washed after, they prove excellent for that use; that is, being fried with yolk of eggs, the flowers of cowslips and of primroses, and a little tansy; thus used they make a dainty dish of meat.

The LOACH is, as I told you, a most dainty fish: he breeds and feeds in little and clear swift brooks or rills, and lives there upon the gravel, and in the sharpest streams: he grows not to be above a finger long, and no thicker than is suitable to that length. The Loach is not unlike the shape of the Eel: he has a beard or wattles like a barbel. He has two fins at his sides, four at his belly, and one at his tail; he is dappled with many black or brown spots; his mouth is barbel-like under his nose.

This fish is usually full of eggs or spawn; and is by Gesner, and other learned physicians, commended for great nourishment, and to be very grateful both to the palate and stomach of sick persons. He is to be fished for with a very small worm, at the bottom; for he very seldom, or never, rises above the gravel, on which I told you he usually gets his living.

The MILLER'S-THUMB, or BULL-HEAD, is a fish of no pleasing shape. He is by Gesner compared to the Sea-toad-fish, for his similitude and shape. It has a head big and flat, much greater than suitable to his body; a mouth very wide, and usually gaping; he is without teeth, but his lips are very rough, much like to a file. He hath two fins near to his gills, which be roundish or crested; two fins also under the belly; two on the back; one below the vent; and the fin of his tail is round. Nature hath painted the body of this fish with whitish, blackish, brownish spots. They be usually full of eggs or spawn all the summer, I mean the females; and those eggs swell their vents almost into the form of a dug. They begin to spawn about April, and, as I told you, spawn several months in the summer. And in the winter, the Minnow, and Loach, and Bull-head dwell in the mud, as the Eel doth; or we know not where, no more than we know where the cuckoo and swallow, and other half-year birds, which first appear to us in April, spend their six cold, winter, melancholy months. This BULL-HEAD does usually dwell, and hide himself, in holes, or amongst stones in clear water; and in very hot days will lie a long time very still, and sun himself, and will be easy to be seen upon any flat stone, or any gravel; at which time he will suffer an angler to put a hook, baited with a small worm, very near unto his very mouth: and he never refuses to bite, nor indeed to be caught with the worst of anglers. Matthiolus commends him much more for his taste and nourishment, than for his shape or beauty.

There is also a little fish called a STICKLEBAG, a fish without scales, but hath his body fenced with several prickles. I know not where he dwells in winter; nor what he is good for in summer, but only to make sport for boys and women-anglers, and to feed other fish that be fish of prey, as Trouts in particular, who will bite at him as at a Penk; and better, if your hook be rightly baited with him, for he may be so baited as, his tail turning like the sail of a wind-mill, will make him turn more quick than any Penk or Minnow can. For note, that the nimble turning of that, or the Minnow is the perfection of Minnow-fishing. To which end, if you put your hook into his mouth, and out at his tail; and then, having first tied him with white thread a little above his tail, and placed him after such a manner on your hook as he is like to turn then sew up his mouth to your line, and he is like to turn quick, and tempt any Trout: but if he does not turn quick, then turn his tail, a little more or less, towards the inner part, or towards the side of the hook; or put the Minnow or Sticklebag a little more crooked or more straight on your hook, until it will turn both true and fast; and then doubt not but to tempt any great Trout that lies in a swift stream. And the Loach that I told you of will do the like: no bait is more tempting, provided the Loach be not too big.

And now, scholar, with the help of this fine morning, and your patient attention, I have said all that my present memory will afford me, concerning most of the several fish that are usually fished for in fresh waters.

VENATOR. But, master, you have by your former civility made me hope that you will make good your promise, and say something of the several rivers that be of most note in this nation; and also of fish-ponds, and the ordering of them: and do it I pray, good master; for I love any discourse of rivers, and fish and fishing; the time spent in such discourse passes away very pleasantly.

# THE FIFTH DAY—*continued*

## *Of Rivers, and some Observations of Fish*

### CHAPTER XIX

PISCATOR

WELL, scholar, since the ways and weather do both favour us, and that we yet see not Tottenham-Cross, you shall see my willingness to satisfy your desire. And, first, for the rivers of this nation: there be, as you may note out of Dr. Heylin's *Geography* and others, in number three hundred and twenty-five; but those of chiefest note he reckons and describes as followeth.

The chief is THAMISIS, compounded of two rivers, Thame and Isis; whereof the former, rising somewhat beyond Thame in Buckinghamshire, and the latter near Cirencester in Gloucestershire, meet together about Dorchester in Oxfordshire; the issue of which happy conjunction is Thamisis, or Thames; hence it flieth betwixt Berks, Buckinghamshire, Middlesex, Surrey, Kent, and Essex: and so weddeth itself to the Kentish Medway, in the very jaws of the ocean. This glorious river feeleth the violence and benefit of the sea more than any river in Europe; ebbing and flowing, twice a day, more than sixty miles; about whose banks are so many fair towns and princely palaces, that a German poet thus truly spake:

*Tot campos, &c.*

We saw so many woods and princely bowers,
Sweet fields, brave palaces, and stately towers;
So many gardens drest with curious care,
That Thames with royal Tiber may compare.

2. The second river of note is SABRINA or SEVERN: it hath its beginning in Plinilimmon-hill, in Montgomeryshire; and his end seven miles from Bristol; washing, in the mean space, the walls of Shrewsbury, Worcester, and Gloucester, and divers other places and palaces of note.

3. TRENT, so called from thirty kind of fishes that are found in it, or for that it receiveth thirty lesser rivers; who having his fountain in Staffordshire, and gliding through the counties of Nottingham, Lincoln, Leicester, and York, augmenteth the turbulent current of Humber, the most violent stream of all the isle. This Humber is not, to say truth, a distinct river having a spring-head of his own, but it is rather the mouth or *æstuarium* of divers rivers here confluent and meeting together, namely, your Derwent, and especially of Ouse and Trent; and, as the Danow, having received into its channel the river Dravus, Savus, Tibiscus, and divers others, changeth his name into this of *Humberabus*, as the old geographers call it.

4. MEDWAY, a Kentish river, famous for harbouring the royal navy.

5. TWEED, the north-east bound of England; on whose northern banks is seated the strong and impregnable town of Berwick.

6. TYNE, famous for Newcastle, and her inexhaustible coal-pits. These, and the rest of principal note, are thus comprehended in one of Mr. Drayton's Sonnets:

Our floods' queen, Thames, for ships and swans is crown'd;
And stately Severn for her shore is prais'd;
The crystal Trent, for fords and fish renown'd;
And Avon's fame to Albion's cliffs is rais'd.

Carlegion Chester vaunts her holy Dee;
York many wonders of her Ouse can tell;
The Peak, her Dove, whose banks so fertile be,
And Kent will say her Medway doth excel:

Cotswold commends her Isis to the Tame;
Our northern borders boast of Tweed's fair flood;
Our Western parts extol their Willy's fame,
And the old Lea brags of the Danish blood.

These observations are out of learned Dr. Heylin, and my old deceased friend, Michael Drayton; and because you say you love such discourses as these, of rivers, and fish, and fishing, I love you the better, and love the more to impart them to you. Nevertheless, scholar, if I should begin but to name the several sorts of strange fish that are usually taken in many of those rivers that run into the sea, I might beget wonder in you, or unbelief, or both: and yet I will venture to tell you a real truth concerning one lately dissected by Dr. Wharton, a man of great learning and experience, and of equal freedom to communicate it; one that loves me and my art; one to whom I have been beholden for many of the choicest observations that I have imparted to you. This good man, that dares do anything rather than tell an untruth, did, I say, tell me he had lately dissected one strange fish, and he thus described it to me:

"This fish was almost a yard broad, and twice that length; his mouth wide enough to receive, or take into it, the head of a man; his stomach, seven or eight inches broad. He is of a slow motion; and usually lies or lurks close in the mud; and has a moveable string on his head, about a span or near unto a quarter of a yard long; by the moving of which, which is his natural bait, when he lies close and unseen in the mud, he draws other smaller fish so close to him, that he can suck them into his mouth, and so devours and digests them."

And, scholar, do not wonder at this; for besides the credit of the relator, you are to note, many of these, and fishes which are of the like and more unusual shapes, are very often taken on the mouths of our sea rivers, and on the sea shore. And this will be no wonder to any that have travelled Egypt; where, 'tis known, the famous river Nilus does not only breed fishes that yet want names, but, by the overflowing of that river, and the help of the sun's heat on the fat slime which the river leaves on the banks when it falls back into its natural channel, such strange fish and beasts are also bred, that no man can give a name to; as Grotius in his *Sopham*, and others, have observed.

But whither am I strayed in this discourse. I will end it by telling you, that at the mouth of some of these rivers of ours, Herrings are so plentiful, as namely, near to Yarmouth in Norfolk, and in the west country Pilchers so very plentiful, as you will wonder to read what our learned Camden relates of them in his *Britannia*.

Well, scholar, I will stop here, and tell you what by reading and conference I have observed concerning fish-ponds.

# THE FIFTH DAY—*continued*

## *Of Fish-Ponds*

### CHAPTER XX

PISCATOR

DOCTOR LEBAULT, the learned Frenchman, in his large discourse of *Maison Rustique*, gives this direction for making of fish-ponds. I shall refer you to him, to read it at large: but I think I shall contract it, and yet make it as useful.

He adviseth, that when you have drained the ground, and made the earth firm where the head of the pond must be, that you must then, in that place, drive in two or three rows of oak or elm piles, which should be scorched in the fire, or half-burnt, before they be driven into the earth; for being thus used, it preserves them much longer from rotting. And having done so, lay faggots or bavins of smaller wood betwixt them: and then, earth betwixt and above them: and then, having first very well rammed them and the earth, use another pile in like manner as the first were: and note, that the second pile is to be of or about the height that you intend to make your sluice or floodgate, or the vent that you intend shall convey the overflowings of your pond in any flood that shall endanger the breaking of your pond-dam.

Then he advises, that you plant willows or owlers, about it, or both: and then cast in bavins, in some places not far from the side, and in the most sandy places, for fish both to spawn upon, and to defend them and the young fry from the many fish, and also from vermin, that lie at watch to destroy them, especially the spawn of the Carp and Tench, when 'tis left to the mercy of ducks or vermin.

He, and Dubravius, and all others advise, that you make choice of such a place for your pond, that it may be refreshed with a little rill, or with rain water, running or falling into it; by which fish are more inclined both to breed, and are also refreshed and fed the better, and do prove to be of a much sweeter and more pleasant taste.

To which end it is observed, that such pools as be large and have most gravel, and shallows where fish may sport themselves, do afford fish of the purest taste. And note, that in all pools it is best for fish to have some retiring place; as namely, hollow banks, or shelves, or roots of trees, to keep them from danger, and, when they think fit, from the extreme heat of summer; as also from the extremity of cold in winter. And note, that if many trees be growing about your pond, the leaves thereof falling into the water, make it nauseous to the fish, and the fish to be so to the eater of it.

'Tis noted, that the Tench and Eel love mud; and the Carp loves gravelly ground, and in the hot months to feed on grass. You are to cleanse your pond, if you intend either profit or pleasure, once every three or four years, especially some ponds, and then let it dry six or twelve months, both to kill the water-weeds, as water-lilies, can-docks, reate, and bulrushes, that breed there; and also that as these die for want of water, so grass may grow in the pond's bottom, which Carps will eat greedily in all the hot months, if the pond be clean. The letting your pond dry and sowing oats in the bottom is also good, for the fish feed the faster; and being sometimes let dry, you may observe what kind of fish either increases or thrives best in that water; for they differ much, both in their breeding and feeding.

Lebault also advises, that if your ponds be not very large and roomy, that you often feed your fish, by throwing into them chippings of bread, curds, grains, or the entrails of chickens or of any fowl or beast that you kill to feed yourselves; for these afford fish a great relief. He says, that frogs and ducks do much harm, and devour both the spawn and the young fry of all fish, especially of the Carp; and I have, besides experience, many testimonies of it. But Lebault allows water-frogs to be good meat, especially in some months, if they be fat: but you are to note, that he is a Frenchman; and we English will hardly believe him, though we know frogs are usually eaten in his country: however he advises to destroy them and king-fishers out of your ponds. And he advises not to suffer much shooting at wild fowl; for that, he says, affrightens, and harms, and destroys the fish.

Note, that Carps and Tench thrive and breed best when no other fish is put with them into the same pond; for all other fish devour their spawn, or at least the greatest part of it. And note, that clods of grass thrown into any pond feed any Carps in summer; and that garden-earth and parsley thrown into a pond recovers and refreshes the sick fish. And note, that when you store your pond, you are to put into it two or three melters for one spawner, if you put them into a breeding-pond; but if into a nurse-pond, or feeding-pond, in which they will not breed, then no care is to be taken whether there be most male or female Carps.

It is observed that the best ponds to breed Carps are those that be stony or sandy, and are warm, and free from wind; and that are not deep, but have willow-trees and grass on their sides, over which the water does sometimes flow: and note, that Carps do more usually breed in marle-pits, or pits that have clean clay bottoms; or in new ponds, or ponds that lie dry a winter season, than in old ponds that be full of mud and weeds.

Well, Scholar, I have told you the substance of all that either observation or discourse, or a diligent survey of Dubravius and Lebault hath told me: not that they, in their long discourses, have not said more; but the most of the rest are so common observations, as if a man should tell a good arithmetician that twice two is four. I will therefore put an end to this discourse; and we will here sit down and rest us.

# THE FIFTH DAY—*continued*

## CHAPTER XXI

### PISCATOR AND VENATOR

PISCATOR. Well, Scholar, I have held you too long about these cadis, and smaller fish, and rivers, and fish-ponds; and my spirits are almost spent, and so I doubt is your patience; but being we are now almost at Tottenham where I first met you, and where we are to part, I will lose no time, but give you a little direction how to make and order your lines, and to colour the hair of which you make your lines, for that is very needful to be known of an angler; and also how to paint your rod, especially your top; for a right-grown top is a choice commodity, and should be preserved from the water soaking into it, which makes it in wet weather to be heavy and fish ill-favouredly, and not true; and also it rots quickly for want of painting: and I think a good top is worth preserving, or I had not taken care to keep a top above twenty years.

But first for your Line. First note, that you are to take care that your hair be round and clear, and free from galls, or scabs, or frets: for a well-chosen, even, clear, round hair, of a kind of glass-colour, will prove as strong as three uneven scabby hairs that are ill-chosen, and full of galls or unevenness. You shall seldom find a black hair but it is round, but many white are flat and uneven; therefore, if you get a lock of right, round, clear, glass-colour hair, make much of it.

And for making your line, observe this rule: first, let your hair be clean washed ere you go about to twist it; and then choose not only the clearest hair for it, but hairs that be of an equal bigness, for such do usually stretch all together, and break all together, which hairs of an unequal bigness never do, but break singly, and so deceive the angler that trusts to them.

When you have twisted your links, lay them in water for a quarter of an hour at least, and then twist them over again before you tie them into a line: for those that do not so shall usually find their line to have a hair or two shrink, and be shorter than the rest, at the first fishing with it, which is so much of the strength of the line lost for want of first watering it, and then re-twisting it; and this is most visible in a seven-hair line, one of those which hath always a black hair in the middle.

And for dyeing of your hairs, do it thus: take a pint of strong ale, half a pound of soot, and a little quantity of the juice of walnut-tree leaves, and an equal quantity of alum: put these together into a pot, pan, or pipkin, and boil them half an hour; and having so done, let it cool; and being cold, put your hair into it, and there let it lie; it will turn your hair to be a kind of water or glass colour, or greenish; and the longer you let it lie, the deeper coloured it will be. You might be taught to make many other colours, but it is to little purpose; for doubtless the water-colour or glass-coloured hair is the most choice and most useful for an angler, but let it not be too green.

But if you desire to colour hair greener, then do it thus: take a quart of small ale, half a pound of alum; then put these into a pan or pipkin, and your hair into it with them; then put it upon a fire, and let it boil softly for half an hour; and then take out your hair, and let it dry; and having so done, then take a pottle of water, and put into it two handfuls of marigolds, and cover it with a tile or what you think fit, and set it again on the fire, where it is to boil again softly for half an hour, about which time the scum will turn yellow; then put into it half a pound of copperas, beaten small, and with it the hair that you intend to colour; then let the hair be boiled softly till half the liquor be wasted, and then let it cool three or four hours, with your hair in it; and you are to observe that the more copperas you put into it, the greener it will be; but doubtless the pale green is best. But if you desire yellow hair, which is only good when the weeds rot, then put in more marigolds; and abate most of the copperas, or leave it quite out, and take a little verdigris instead of it.

This for colouring your hair.

And as for painting your Rod, which must be in oil, you must first make a size with glue and water, boiled together until the glue be dissolved, and the size of a lye-colour: then strike your size upon the wood with a bristle, or a brush or pencil, whilst it is hot: that being quite dry, take white-lead, and a little red-lead, and a little coal-black, so much as altogether will make an ash-colour: grind these altogether with linseed-oil; let it be thick, and lay it thin upon the wood with a brush or pencil: this do for the ground of any colour to lie upon wood.

For a green, take pink and verdigris, and grind them together in linseed oil, as thin as you can well grind it: then lay it smoothly on with your brush, and drive it thin; once doing, for the most part, will serve, if you lay it well; and if twice, be sure your first colour be thoroughly dry before you lay on a second.

Well, Scholar, having now taught you to paint your rod, and we having still a mile to Tottenham High-Cross, I will, as we walk towards it in the cool shade of this sweet honeysuckle hedge, mention to you some of the thoughts and joys that have possessed my soul since we two met together. And these thoughts shall be told you, that you also may join with me in thankfulness to the Giver of every good and perfect gift, for our happiness. And that our present happiness may appear to be the greater, and we the more thankful for it, I will beg you to consider with me how many do, even at this very time, lie under the torment of the stone, the gout, and tooth-ache; and this we are free from. And every misery that I miss is a new mercy; and therefore let us be thankful. There have been, since we met, others that have met disasters or broken limbs; some have been blasted, others thunder-strucken: and we have been freed from these, and all those many other miseries that threaten human nature; let us therefore rejoice and be thankful. Nay, which is a far greater mercy, we are free from the insupportable burthen of an accusing tormenting conscience; a misery that none can bear: and therefore let us praise Him for His preventing grace, and say, Every misery that I miss is a new mercy. Nay, let me tell you, there be many that have forty times our estates, that would give the greatest part of it to be healthful and cheerful like us, who, with the expense of a little money, have eat and drunk, and laughed, and angled, and sung, and slept securely; and rose next day and cast away care, and sung, and laughed, and angled again; which are blessings rich men cannot purchase with all their money. Let me tell you, Scholar, I have a rich neighbour that is always so busy that he has no leisure to laugh; the whole business of his life is to get money, and more money, that he may still get more and more money; he is still drudging on, and says, that Solomon says, "The diligent hand maketh rich"; and it is true indeed: but he considers not that it is not in the power of riches to make a man happy; for it was wisely said, by a man of great observation, "That there be as many miseries beyond riches as on this side of them." And yet God deliver us from pinching poverty; and grant, that having a competency, we may be content and thankful. Let not us repine, or so much as think the gifts of God unequally dealt, if we see another abound with riches; when, as God knows, the cares that are the keys that keep those riches hang often so heavily at the rich man's girdle, that they clog him with weary days and restless nights, even when others sleep quietly. We see but the outside of the rich man's happiness: few consider him to be like the silk-worm, that, when she seems to play, is, at the very same time, spinning her own bowels, and consuming herself; and this many rich men do, loading themselves with corroding cares, to keep what they have, probably, unconscionably got. Let us, therefore, be thankful for health and a competence; and above all, for a quiet conscience.

Let me tell you, Scholar, that Diogenes walked on a day, with his friend, to see a country fair; where he saw ribbons, and looking-glasses, and nutcrackers, and fiddles, and hobby-horses, and many other gimcracks; and, having observed them, and all the other finnimbruns that make a complete country-fair, he said to his friend, "Lord, how many things are there in this world of which Diogenes hath no need!" And truly it is so, or might be so, with very many who vex and toil themselves to get what they have no need of. Can any man charge God, that He hath not given him enough to make his life happy? No, doubtless; for nature is content with a little. And yet you shall hardly meet with a man that complains not of some want; though he, indeed, wants nothing but his will; it may be, nothing but his will of his poor neighbour, for not worshipping, or not flattering him: and thus, when we might be happy and quiet, we create trouble to ourselves. I have heard of a man that was angry with himself because he was no taller; and of a woman that broke her looking-glass because it would not shew her face to be as young and handsome as her next neighbour's was. And I knew another to whom God had given health and plenty; but a wife that nature had made peevish, and her husband's riches had made purse-proud; and must, because she was rich, and for no other virtue, sit in the highest pew in the church; which being denied her, she engaged her husband into a contention for it, and at last into a law-suit with a dogged neighbour who was as rich as he, and had a wife as peevish and purse-proud as the other: and this law-suit begot higher oppositions, and actionable words, and more vexations and lawsuits; for you must remember that both were rich, and must therefore have their wills. Well! this wilful, purse-proud law-suit lasted during the life of the first husband; after which his wife vext and chid, and chid and vext, till she also chid and vext herself into her grave: and so the wealth of these poor rich people was curst into a punishment, because they wanted meek and thankful hearts; for those only can make us happy. I knew a man that had health and riches; and several houses, all beautiful, and ready furnished; and would often trouble himself and family to be removing from one house to another: and being asked by a friend why he removed so often from one house to another, replied, "It was to find content in some one of them." But his friend, knowing his temper, told him, "If he would find content in any of his houses, he must leave himself behind him; for content will never dwell but in a meek and quiet soul." And this may appear, if we read and consider what our Saviour says in St. Matthew's Gospel; for He there says—"Blessed be the merciful, for they shall obtain mercy. Blessed be the pure in heart, for they shall see God. Blessed be the poor in spirit, for theirs is the kingdom of heaven. And, Blessed be the meek, for they shall possess the earth." Not that the meek shall not also obtain mercy, and see God, and be comforted, and at last come to the kingdom of heaven: but in the meantime, he, and he only, possesses the earth, as he goes towards that kingdom of heaven, by being humble and cheerful, and content with what his good God had allotted him. He has no turbulent, repining, vexatious thoughts that he deserves better; nor is vext when he see others possest of more honour or more riches than his wise God has allotted for his share: but he possesses what he has with a meek and contented quietness, such a quietness as makes his very dreams pleasing, both to God and himself.

My honest Scholar, all this is told to incline you to thankfulness; and to incline you the more, let me tell you, and though the prophet David was guilty of murder and adultery, and many other of the most deadly sins, yet he was said to be a man after God's own heart, because he abounded more with thankfulness that any other that is mentioned in holy scripture, as may appear in his book of Psalms; where there is such a commixture, of his confessing of his sins and unworthiness, and such thankfulness for God's pardon and mercies, as did make him to be accounted, even by God himself, to be a man after his own heart: and let us, in that, labour to be as like him as we can; let not the blessings we receive daily from God make us not to value, or not praise Him, because they be common; let us not forget to praise Him for the innocent mirth and pleasure we have met with since we met together. What would a blind man give to see the pleasant rivers, and meadows, and flowers, and fountains, that we have met with since we met together? I have been told, that if a man that was born blind could obtain to have his sight for but only one hour during his whole life, and should, at the first opening of his eyes, fix his sight upon the sun when it was in its full glory, either at the rising or setting of it, he would be so transported and amazed, and so admire the glory of it, that he would not willingly turn his eyes from that first ravishing object, to behold all the other various beauties this world could present to him. And this, and many other like blessings, we enjoy daily. And for the most of them, because they be so common, most men forget to pay their praises: but let not us; because it is a sacrifice so pleasing to Him that made that sun and us, and still protects us, and gives us flowers, and showers, and stomachs, and meat, and content, and leisure to go a-fishing.

Well, Scholar, I have almost tired myself, and, I fear, more than almost tired you. But I now see Tottenham High-Cross; and our short walk thither shall put a period to my too long discourse; in which my meaning was, and is, to plant that in your mind with which I labour to possess my own soul; that is, a meek and thankful heart. And to that end

I have shewed you, that riches without them, do not make any man happy. But let me tell you, that riches with them remove many fears and cares. And therefore my advice is, that you endeavour to be honestly rich, or contentedly poor: but be sure that your riches be justly got, or you spoil all. For it is well said by Caussin, "He that loses his conscience has nothing left that is worth keeping." Therefore be sure you look to that. And, in the next place, look to your health: and if you have it, praise God, and value it next to a good conscience; for health is the second blessing that we mortals are capable of; a blessing that money cannot buy; and therefore value it, and be thankful for it. As for money, which may be said to be the third blessing, neglect it not: but note, that there is no necessity of being rich; for I told you, there be as many miseries beyond riches as on this side them: and if you have a competence, enjoy it with a meek, cheerful, thankful heart. I will tell you, Scholar, I have heard a grave Divine say, that God has two dwellings; one in heaven, and the other in a meek and thankful heart; which Almighty God grant to me, and to my honest Scholar. And so you are welcome to Tottenham High-Cross.

VENATOR. Well, Master, I thank you for all your good directions; but for none more than this last, of thankfulness, which I hope I shall never forget. And pray let's now rest ourselves in this sweet shady arbour, which nature herself has woven with her own fine fingers; 'tis such a contexture of woodbines, sweetbriar, jasmine, and myrtle; and so interwoven, as will secure us both from the sun's violent heat, and from the approaching shower. And being set down, I will requite a part of your courtesies with a bottle of sack, milk, oranges, and sugar, which, all put together, make a drink like nectar; indeed, too good for any but us Anglers. And so, Master, here is a full glass to you of that liquor: and when you have pledged me, I will repeat the Verses which I promised you: it is a Copy printed among some of Sir Henry Wotton's, and doubtless made either by him, or by a lover of angling. Come, Master, now drink a glass to me, and then I will pledge you, and fall to my repetition; it is a description of such country recreations as I have enjoyed since I had the happiness to fall into your company.

Quivering fears, heart-tearing cares,
Anxious sighs, untimely tears,
  Fly, fly to courts,
  Fly to fond worldlings' sports,
Where strain'd sardonic smiles are glosing still,
And Grief is forc'd to laugh against her will:
  Where mirth's but mummery,
  And sorrows only real be.

Fly from our country pastimes, fly,
Sad troops of human misery.
  Come, serene looks,
  Clear as the crystal brooks,
Or the pure azur'd heaven that smiles to see
The rich attendance of our poverty:
  Peace and a secure mind,
  Which all men seek, we only find.

Abused mortals! did you know
Where joy, heart's-ease, and comforts grow,
  You'd scorn proud towers,
  And seek them in these bowers;
Where winds, sometimes, our woods perhaps may shake,
But blust'ring care could never tempest make,
  Nor murmurs e'er come nigh us,
  Saving of fountains that glide by us.

Here's no fantastick mask, nor dance,
But of our kids that frisk and prance;
  Nor wars are seen
  Unless upon the green
Two harmless lambs are butting one the other,
Which done, both bleating run, each to his mother
  And wounds are never found,
  Save what the plough-share gives the ground.

Here are no false entrapping baits,
To hasten too, too hasty Fates,
  Unless it be
  The fond credulity
Of silly fish, which worldling like, still look
Upon the bait, but never on the hook;
  Nor envy, unless among
  The birds, for prize of their sweet song.

Go, let the diving negro seek
For gems, hid in some forlorn creek:
  We all pearls scorn,
  Save what the dewy morn
Congeals upon each little spire of grass,
Which careless shepherds beat down as they pass:
  And gold ne'er here appears,
  Save what the yellow Ceres bears.

Blest silent groves, oh may ye be,
For ever, mirth's best nursery!
  May pure contents
  For ever pitch their tents

Upon these downs, these meads, these rocks, these mountains,
And peace still slumber by these purling fountains:
  Which we may, every year,
  Meet when we come a-fishing here.

PISCATOR. Trust me, Scholar, I thank you heartily for these Verses: they be choicely good, and doubtless made by a lover of angling. Come, now, drink a glass to me, and I will requite you with another very good copy: it is a farewell to the vanities of the world, and some say written by Sir Harry Wotton, who I told you was an excellent angler. But let them be writ by whom they will, he that writ them had a brave soul, and must needs be possest with happy thoughts at the time of their composure.

Farewell, ye gilded follies, pleasing troubles;
Farewell, ye honour'd rags, ye glorious bubbles;
Fame's but a hollow echo; Gold, pure clay;
Honour the darling but of one short day;
Beauty, th' eye's idol, but a damask'd skin;
State, but a golden prison, to live in
And torture free-born minds; embroider'd Trains,
Merely but pageants for proud swelling veins;
And Blood allied to greatness is alone
Inherited, not purchas'd, nor our own.
  Fame, Honour, Beauty, State, Train, Blood and Birth,
  Are but the fading blossoms of the earth.

I would be great, but that the sun doth still
Level his rays against the rising hill:
I would be high, but see the proudest oak
Most subject to the rending thunder-stroke:
I would be rich, but see men, too unkind,
Dig in the bowels of the richest mind:
I would be wise, but that I often see
The fox suspected, whilst the ass goes free:
I would be fair, but see the fair and proud,
Like the bright sun, oft setting in a cloud:
I would be poor, but know the humble grass
Still trampled on by each unworthy ass:
Rich, hated; wise, suspected; scorn'd if poor;
Great, fear'd; fair, tempted; high, still envy'd more.
  I have wish'd all; but now I wish for neither,
  Great, high, rich, wise, nor fair: poor I'll be rather.

Would the World now adopt me for her heir;
Would beauty's Queen entitle me the fair;
Fame speak me fortune's minion; could I "vie
Angels" with India; with a speaking eye

Command bare heads, bow'd knees; strike justice dumb,
As well as blind and lame; or give a tongue
To stones by epitaphs; be call'd "great master"
In the loose rhymes of every poetaster?
Could I be more than any man that lives,
Great, fair, rich, wise, all in superlatives;
Yet I more freely would these gifts resign,
Than ever fortune would have made them mine;
  And hold one minute of this holy leisure
  Beyond the riches of this empty pleasure.

Welcome, pure thoughts; welcome, ye silent groves;
These guests, these courts, my soul most dearly loves.
Now the wing'd people of the sky shall sing
My cheerful anthems to the gladsome spring:
A pray'r-book, now, shall be my looking-glass,
In which I will adore sweet virtue's face.
Here dwell no hateful looks, no palace cares,
No broken vows dwell here, nor pale-fac'd fears;
Then here I'll sit, and sigh my hot love's folly,
And learn t' affect an holy melancholy:
  And if contentment be a stranger then,
  I'll ne'er look for it, but in heaven, again.

VENATOR. Well, Master, these verses be worthy to keep a room in every man's memory. I thank you for them; and I thank you for your many instructions, which, God willing, I will not forget. And as St. Austin, in his *Confessions*, commemorates the kindness of his friend Verecundus, for lending him and his companion a country house, because there they rested and enjoyed themselves, free from the troubles of the world, so, having had the like advantage, both by your conversation and the art you have taught me, I ought ever to do the like; for, indeed, your company and discourse have been so useful and pleasant, that, I may truly say, I have only lived since I enjoyed them and turned angler, and not before. Nevertheless, here I must part with you; here in this now sad place, where I was so happy as first to meet you: but I shall long for the ninth of May; for then I hope again to enjoy your beloved company, at the appointed time and place. And now I wish for some somniferous potion, that might force me to sleep away the intermitted time, which will pass away with me as tediously as it does with men in sorrow; nevertheless I will make it as short as I can, by my hopes and wishes: and, my good Master, I will not forget the doctrine which you told me Socrates taught his scholars, that they should not think to be honoured so much for being philosophers, as to honour philosophy by their virtuous lives. You advised me to the like concerning Angling, and

I will endeavour to do so; and to live like those many worthy men, of which you made mention in the former part of your discourse. This is my firm resolution. And as a pious man advised his friend, that, to beget mortification, he should frequent churches, and view monuments, and charnel-houses, and then and there consider how many dead bodies time had piled up at the gates of death, so when I would beget content, and increase confidence in the power, and wisdom, and providence of Almighty God, I will walk the meadows, by some gliding stream, and there contemplate the lilies that take no care, and those very many other various little living creatures that are not only created, but fed, man knows not how, by the goodness of the God of Nature, and therefore trust in him. This is my purpose; and so, let everything that hath breath praise the Lord: and let the blessing of St. Peter's Master be with mine.

PISCATOR. And upon all that are lovers of virtue; and dare trust in his providence; and be quiet; and go a Angling.

"Study to be quiet."

THE END